LAW
AND
DISORDER

How a Kid from the Bronx
Became America's
Top Drug Prosecutor

ROBERT H. SILBERING

North Carolina

Law and Disorder: How a Kid from the Bronx Became America's Top Drug Prosecutor
© 2024 Robert H. Silbering. All rights reserved.

This story is told from the author's experience and perspective.

Published in the United States by WriteLife Publishing
(An imprint of Boutique of Quality Books Publishing Company)
www.writelife.com

978-1-60808-296-4 (p)
978-1-60808-295-7 (e)

Library of Congress Control Number: 2023951224

Book design by Robin Krauss, www.bookformatters.com
Cover design by Rebecca Lown, www.rebeccalowndesign.com

First Editor: Caleb Guard
Second Editor: Allison Itterly

PRAISE FOR
LAW AND DISORDER
AND ROBERT H. SILBERING

"I knew, respected and worked with Bob Silbering in the family court in the 70s. We were both prosecutors. The justice system was trying to find its legs. A mix of good judges and bad. Good lawyers and bad. Some dedicated. Some not. Bob was one of the dedicated ones. He chronicles the justice system with impeccable recall in this book. Sadly, the more things change, the more they stay the same. The system has not learned from history. Read this book and you'll understand."

— Judge Judy Sheindlin

"*Law and Disorder* chronicles Bob Silbering's extraordinary and unparalleled career as a prosecutor for many decades successfully battling the dual plagues of rising crime and drug fueled violence and disorder that threatened to overwhelm New York City. Silbering takes you on a high-speed roller coaster ride through those turbulent and exciting times, recounting his experiences working for the legendary Manhattan DA Bob Morgenthau and then as the Special Narcotics Prosecutor for New York City as they confronted many of the crime stories that dominated the front pages of NYC's famous tabloids. It's a must read. You won't be disappointed."

— Bill Bratton, Former New York City Police Commissioner (1994-1996, 2014-2016)

"Bob Silbering had a front row seat directing the prosecution of major international drug dealers who were destroying the quality of life in New York City. His 'low key' style and 'easy going' personality allowed him to move seamlessly and effectively among the many levels of law enforcement: federal, state, and local.

Bob's story is a New York City story where hard work, a sense of humor and determination will position you to succeed. This is a must read for everybody interested in drug enforcement and the criminal justice system in New York City."

— Lew Rice, Former DEA Special Agent in Charge,
New York Division (1997-2001)

Law and Disorder is a must read for prosecutors and law enforcement leaders alike charged with tackling today's most pressing and complex issues. Pursuing justice is a team sport and Bob was the quintessential coach who brought the best players together to work collaboratively and effectively to bring criminals to justice. As a former Assistant District Attorney and FBI special agent, I am forever indebted to Bob for his leadership and wisdom."

— Michael C. McGarrity, Assistant Director Counterterrorism,
FBI (Retired); Director of Counterterrorism,
White House National Security Council (Retired)

To my family for all your love and support.
You're the best!

ACKNOWLEDGMENTS

First and foremost I would like to thank my chief editor, advisor, and wife Shelley for all her help, patience, and support in getting this book written. She was always there when I needed her guidance and wisdom in completing the project. I also want to thank my daughter Jill and son David and their spouses Scott and Jackie for all their support and encouragement. A special thanks to Gil Reavill for helping me write and structure the book and bring all my memories and stories that went into this book to life. Without his encouragement and experience this book would never have been written.

Accuracy was very important to me in writing this book. I would like to thank the following wonderful people who helped to refresh my recollection and add details to events that occurred many years ago:

Edward Beach
Bridget Brennan
Patrick Conlon
Steven Fishner
Steven Gutstein
Judge Sterling Johnson
Gary Katz
Jose Maldonado
Mari Maloney
Chris Marzuk
Matthew Menchel

Eric Pomerantz
Jeffrey Schlanger
Judge Robert Seewald
Judge Leslie Crocker Snyder
Jerry Speziale
Ida Van Lindt

I would also like to thank Barry Marin for his technological assistance in helping me get the photo section together.

TABLE OF CONTENTS

"The prosecutor has more control over life, liberty, and reputation than any other person in America."

– *Robert H. Jackson, U.S. Supreme Court Justice*

CHAPTER 1

A KILLING IN QUEENS

On the early morning of February 26, 1988, a rookie NYPD officer named Edward Byrne was parked in his radio patrol car. The block of Inwood Street in South Jamaica, Queens, had become infested with drug crews selling crack, a form of purified cocaine that had the entire city in its deadly grip.

A Guyanese immigrant, who went by the single name of Arjune, lived in a gray clapboard house at Inwood Street and 107th Avenue. An upstanding citizen, he had resisted the plague of narcotics trafficking in the neighborhood. But he'd paid for his bravery, as his home had been firebombed twice. One time, he picked up a flaming Molotov cocktail and tossed it back at his attackers, severely burning his hands in the process.

Still, Arjune didn't back down. He was set to testify against the drug lords who were threatening his life and disrupting the peace on his block.

To protect the witness, the command at the 103rd Precinct in Queens assigned round-the-clock surveillance on Arjune's home, which was why the rookie cop was stationed on the corner of Inwood and 107th that night.

Byrne, the son of a cop, had celebrated his twenty-second birthday only four days before. Relieving Officer Nancy Stefan a little after midnight, he climbed into the driver's seat of the marked Ford Impala squad car and battled boredom during the early morning hours of that cold, cloudy night.

Two gunmen crept up on Byrne's radio car, acting on the orders of their boss, a drug kingpin named Howard "Pappy" Mason, who was intent on intimidating not only Arjune but also the entire NYPD.

One of the gunmen, Todd Scott, tapped on Byrne's passenger side window. Startled, the rookie cop turned his head, instinctively placing his right hand on the duty gun in his belt.

"I'll come around," Todd Scott mumbled, attempting to distract Bryne.

At the same instant, the other gunman, David McClary, sneaked up on the driver's side, leveled a chrome-plated .38 revolver eight inches from Byrne's head, and fired.

The window glass shattered, sending splinters into the rookie's face. The copper-jacketed bullet ripped into Byrne's jaw. McClary kept shooting. Four more bullets effectively destroyed the skull of Officer Edward Byrne, tragically ending his young life.

The duo boasted about the murder as they fled from the scene.

"That shit was swift," crowed Todd Scott.

"I seen his blue eyes," said McClary.

I wasn't there.

The words spoken by the murderers of Officer Edward Byrne were documented from a trial transcript. The facts of the crime were established only in its aftermath in a court of law. This is my world—the justice system—where we seek to determine what actually happened in all criminal matters, large and small. Officer Byrne was one of the many people whose victimhood cried out for vindication. As a prosecutor in New York City, I came to know this story and thousands of others throughout my career.

My professional life was devoted to establishing truth in this admittedly flawed and imperfect system of justice. To paraphrase Winston Churchill's famous line about democracy, the system of judge and jury is the worst form of justice there is, except for all the others that have been tried.

Why am I bringing up a murder that took place decades ago? What possible relevance could such a crime hold in the present day? Who now recalls the name Edward Byrne?

I remember. A lot of other people remember too. When Edward Byrne was assassinated in cold blood, I was serving in the Office of the Special Narcotics Prosecutor in New York City. The city was in a terrible state back then, plagued by chaos on the streets, and ordinary citizens lived in fear.

I spent almost twenty-five years as a prosecutor in New York City, and I learned all about crime, violence, drug abuse, the criminal justice system, and the people who break the law. I faced off with some of the worst examples of humankind. At the same time, I was working with the best and most dedicated prosecutors and law enforcement officers in the country, tasked with the job of ensuring public safety.

For seven years, I held the position of the New York City Special Narcotics Prosecutor, heading up the only office in the nation solely dedicated to investigating and prosecuting felony drug cases. Prior to that role, I had worked for seven years as the Chief Assistant in Special Narcotics, and before that, I spent a decade as an Assistant District Attorney with the Manhattan District Attorney's office, the country's premier prosecutor's office.

But before all that, I came from rather humble beginnings.

CHAPTER 2

MY HUMBLE BEGINNINGS

B oth sets of my grandparents came to the United States with the hope of escaping poverty and the pogroms they faced as Jews in Russia. My paternal grandparents and their three-month-old son, Morris, my father, left Russia in 1907 and somehow got to Southampton, England, where they boarded the *HMS Saxonia* and headed to Boston. Eventually, they made their way to the Lower East Side of Manhattan before finally settling in Brooklyn. My mother's family came from a town in Russia known as Kalmica, or Kalmykia. It was a small town straight out of *Fiddler on the Roof.* Most of my mother's family left for the United States around 1912 when she was an infant. My grandmother was one of eight siblings who had made it to America. According to my relatives, four of my grandmother's siblings died in early childhood due to the poor medical care in Russia. My mother's family and some of her aunts and uncles settled in the Bronx. The rest of her family settled in Brooklyn. All my great-uncles worked hard while the mothers took care of the children.

My father was a classic underachiever. Although very bright, he was not very ambitious. He never learned to drive and never made much money in his work as a supervisor for the Miller-Wohl company, which sold women's dresses. After they married, my parents moved in with my grandparents in the Bronx in a three-bedroom apartment on Rochambeau Avenue. My older brother Steven and I shared a bedroom. It was not a good situation because my father never got along with my mother's parents. They resented the fact that my father never tried to move up but settled for a fairly low-paying job.

Aside from my grandparents, everyone liked my dad. He had a good sense of humor, was always polite, and he rarely cursed. He read the newspapers every day and was well versed in politics and current events. He was also a very honest man and would get upset when he read about politicians being convicted of taking bribes or committing other dishonest acts. He always said that most politicians were "crooks." I think it was his dislike of dishonest politicians and other lawbreakers that got me interested in criminal law and prosecuting the bad guys.

My father was the oldest of his four siblings. After finishing high school, he went to work to help support the family and allow his younger siblings to continue their education. One of his brothers, Sam, died in an accident as a teenager when he was riding his bicycle in the street and got hit by a truck. Another brother, Irving, worked for U.S. Customs. My father's sister, Ray, the youngest of the siblings, went to college and got a degree from Brooklyn College. It was unusual for a woman in the 1940s to attend college. She lived a long and happy life and passed away in March 2023, a few weeks shy of her 104th birthday.

My mother, Tessie, was a housewife. She always had a lot of energy, and she needed it to deal with my grandmother, who had no education, spoke barely any English, and loved to get into arguments with people. Tessie was very creative. When she was in her seventies, she started writing poetry about people and places. She composed witty poems about me, my brother, and my kids. She actually submitted a poem to *Reader's Digest* and won a prize for it. She loved being around people and family.

My mother had a sister, Ann, who lived in our apartment house, and a brother, Daniel, who lived in Manhattan. Daniel was a doctor, and was regarded as the prince of the family, mainly because he treated all my relatives for free.

I was born Robert Howard Silbering in the Bronx on June 6, 1947. I have only one sibling, my brother Steven, who is seven years older than me. Steven and I are quite different. My brother was a brilliant student. He graduated from City College and went on to achieve a master's and PhD degree in organic chemistry from Rensselaer Polytech University in upstate New York. He furthered his education at the University of Minnesota with a post-doctoral degree in pharmacology, then went on to a successful career working for a number of pharmaceutical companies. Unlike me, he did not have an outgoing personality or a big interest in sports. We were members of the same family, but we had very little in common. My mother always raved about how smart my brother was and that he was an excellent student. She continually asked me why I couldn't be more like him and study and get good grades. She was thrilled when he got his PhD and proudly referred to him as " My son, the doctor."

We never did very much as a family. We never went out to eat, and we didn't own a car. The only vacations we ever took were to the Catskill Mountains for a week where we stayed at a small hotel called the Youngsville Inn. I was the poorest kid of all my friends. While they went to summer camp, I had to make do with hanging around the schoolyard. Their parents all had cars, and they took trips and ate out. I had to work for everything I had. I worked to pay for college and law school, as well as my first new car, a 1970 Plymouth Barracuda. I was never afraid of hard work.

I never felt disadvantaged. I was a happy kid with lots of friends. I felt lucky to be surrounded by loving parents, lots of friends and relatives, and a neighborhood where I felt like I knew everyone who lived in the apartments and worked in the stores that lined the streets. It was a very comforting feeling.

I was blessed to have a reasonable amount of smarts, a good sense of humor, an excellent memory, and the two most important traits to succeed in life and work: good judgment and common sense. I also had an approachable, down-to-earth personality and got along with everyone. I couldn't afford to be arrogant, and in truth, I had no reason to be arrogant about anything. I had a self-deprecating sense of humor and made people laugh when I made jokes about myself. I never had a big ego and didn't get embarrassed easily. I was not sensitive to criticism and could handle the unkind remarks of others.

School became a home away from home for me, not because of anything that happened in the classroom, but due to the goings-on in the schoolyard. I attended Public School 80 for both elementary and junior high, with a student body that was over fifty percent Jewish. A Public Works Administration building created in the 1930s, the school remains a touchstone of my youth, but not for the classes I took there.

I was attracted to the sports fields in the schoolyard like a magnet. I would hurry out the door of our apartment building, turn right, and after a short walk along Rochambeau Avenue, I was there. Pick-up softball, basketball, and touch football games were always being played. At home, I would watch a lot of sports on TV, and because I lived in the Bronx, the kids I knew were all big Yankee fans.

That was the golden era for the Yankees, with Mickey Mantle, Roger Maris, Whitey Ford, and Yogi Berra, so it was a great time to be a fan of the Bronx Bombers. I had pictures of the players up on the wall in my bedroom. When I went to Yankee Stadium with friends, we usually sat on the top deck behind home plate, paying

$1.30 for a grandstand ticket. I spent a lot of time in the House that Ruth Built.

I took the subway everywhere, including Yankee Stadium and Madison Square Garden. When I was a teenager, my friends and I rode the subway all over the place and never really thought about crime or danger.

In my early days, I wasn't much interested in school. I never had an interest in reading books. Academics didn't mean anything to me. Even when I graduated junior high and went on to nearby DeWitt Clinton High School, I was only excited because Clinton had a history of excellent athletic teams.

DeWitt Clinton was an all-boys high school that was located a short distance from Mosholu Parkway and P.S. 80. Burt Lancaster had gone there, as well as the *Get Smart* actor Don Adams. A guy named Ralph Lifshitz attended Clinton a few years before me, who later changed his name to Ralph Lauren. Many other actors and politicians have gone to Clinton as well.

P.S. 80 might have been majority Jewish, but Clinton in my day was pretty diverse, with many Puerto Rican and African American students making up the seven-thousand student body. I might be looking at the past through rose-colored glasses, but I remember us all getting along pretty well.

Whatever subjects I didn't like, I avoided. I cut geometry all the time because there was nothing I hated more in life than geometry. My truancy got my mother summoned to Clinton to meet with the dean.

"Your son is cutting classes," he informed her. "He's a smart kid, but he's not applying himself."

She was called to these kinds of meetings so often that she became disgusted. "I think I'm in school more than you are!" she shouted at me one day. Back then, I had a baseball card collection that probably would have been worth real money today. She took all my cards and threw them out.

When I graduated from Clinton in 1965, I did not know what career I wanted to pursue. Well, actually I *did* know what I wanted to be in junior high: I wanted to play second base for the Yankees. I gradually came to realize I wasn't in the same league as Mantle, Maris, and the others. It was a hard day when I faced the sobering reality that I just wasn't going to be good enough.

My next passion was to be a sportscaster. From watching Yankee games, I knew the language of sports, the play-calling, the patter, and the routines. I knew how the game was supposed to be played and who all the characters were. Mel Allen, the great Yankees announcer, was who I aspired to be, and I could imitate his style with uncanny accuracy.

But a career in sports broadcasting wasn't in the cards either. My grades were not stellar; they were okay, but not great. I went to the required senior-class interview with the school guidance counselor.

"I can suggest the colleges you should apply to," he said. "Since you don't have the best grades, you're not going to get into City College, and you're probably not going to get into Lehman or Baruch. What about a solid SUNY school like New Paltz? Or maybe you should consider private schools."

In the end, I chose Fairleigh Dickinson University, across the Hudson River from the Bronx in Teaneck, New Jersey. It seemed to me I was simply settling for the best school that would have me, but the school turned out to be a lot more than that.

I came to the realization that I had to take school seriously and not goof off anymore. Fairleigh Dickinson University—affectionately referred to as "Harvard on the Hackensack"—lit a fire under me. I had more or less wandered through high school, but as I started college in 1965, I felt myself emerge from intellectual limbo. I began to get interested in the material I was learning. I managed to finish my freshman year as an A student, a status that I had never achieved in my life. My curiosity about the world woke up. Maybe I had just matured a bit. Everything about studying and learning just seemed to click. It was during my freshman year, after taking a Constitutional Law class, that I started to think about a career in law.

While I was in college, I had virtually no spending money, and my parents certainly had none to give me. A boy with empty pockets needs to work. Thankfully, my uncle Daniel, the doctor, helped me out in that respect. He had a second home in Bridgeville, a small town in the Catskill Mountains near Monticello, New York. During his time in the area, my uncle had met the owner of the Salhara Hotel in nearby Woodbourne. He was able to land me a summer job.

This was the mid-1960s, marking the tail end of the golden age of the Catskill resort culture. The entire region was already dwindling from its peak in the 1950s, when over five hundred hotels, bungalow colonies, and summer camps dotted the landscape of upstate New York. "The Jewish Alps," we called it, and the clientele was, in fact, overwhelmingly made up of Jews from New York City and the larger metropolitan area. Businessmen sent their families to the Catskills to beat the summer heat and would join them for the weekends.

If you've ever seen *Dirty Dancing*, read the Herman Wouk novel *Marjorie Morningstar*, or watched the TV series *The Marvelous Mrs. Maisel*, you might have a good sense of what the scene was like. But the real phenomena was ten times as intense as any writer could portray. It was a different era, the heyday of the Borscht Belt, with nightly entertainment from comics, singers, and dance bands.

In the summer of 1966, at the age of eighteen, I started out as a bellhop, schlepping luggage and on occasion helping out as a busboy in the dining room. The next two years I moved up to be a busboy and a waiter. It was a long workday. I got up at seven in the morning, had a quick breakfast, then helped prepare breakfast for the guests. By the time breakfast finished, it was ten-thirty and time to clean up and set the tables for lunch, which started at one. After a short break in the afternoon, the dinner rush was on at seven o'clock.

I loved the job. I had a great time schmoozing with guests and making good tips. Almost every night after work, the waiters, bellhops, and other staffers went out together. I was in college boy heaven.

After that first summer, the Salhara went out of business—a harbinger of the decline of the Catskill scene. But I was hired at a place called Green Acres the next summer. A year later, in 1968, I was hired as a waiter at Esther Manor hotel.

In 1968 it was the Summer of Love, when the flower child craze was in full bloom, but I was pretty much oblivious. The revolution would have to happen without me. The owner's daughter at Esther Manor was married to the singer Neil Sedaka. That's about as close as I ever got to rock and roll.

That year I was a waiter, and because I had such a good memory, I didn't have to write anything down. I did well in that role. I was able to remember all twenty-four separate orders for three tables of eight. That meant I could be the first waiter in the kitchen and was able to get everything taken care of early on.

The mountain air of the Catskills encouraged relaxed attitudes, the loosening of belts, and the corny comic routines of kosher comedians ("My doctor said I was in terrible shape. I told him, 'I want a second opinion.' He said, 'All right, you're ugly too!'"). Everyone, staffers and guests alike, seemed to be some sort of character.

I had a customer who I always addressed formally as "Mr. Fox." Every day after dinner, he would take me aside.

"Bobby," he said, "firstly, if I can put my finger in this coffee, it's not hot enough. And secondly, do you have an extra steak or lamb chop you can give me to take back to the room for my dog, Tiny?"

He was at the resort for a week, and every evening it was the same routine: hotter coffee and a chop for his pet. When the weekend rolled around, I ran into Mr. Fox for the last time while he was packing up his car and leaving with his wife.

"Hi, Mr. Fox," I said. "Wait. Where's your little dog?"

He grabbed his bulging belly with his hands. "You wanna see Tiny? I'll show you Tiny!" His wife cackled like a banshee and they drove away.

I worked in the Catskills for three years, during summer breaks. I consider it a great, entertaining time of my life, a period that also taught me to be independent. Those summers represented the first time I was really ever away from my family. I also made a few bucks, which helped pay for my education.

In my senior year at Fairleigh Dickinson, I was doing so well that the school granted me a partial scholarship. Majoring in American history and government, I took my degree and graduated with honors.

After I graduated from Fairleigh Dickinson, my first thought was to continue my education and go to law school. But the Vietnam War was raging, and law school offered no protection from being drafted into the military. I was no peacenik, but I didn't want to be used as cannon fodder either.

Luckily, Jeff Cohen, a college classmate I am still close with today, pointed me in the right direction. He told me that educators who taught in underserved neighborhoods could get an exemption from the Selective Service. Following Jeff's lead, I landed a job teaching sixth graders in Paterson, New Jersey, even though I had never taken a single education course in college.

While teaching in Paterson, I got my first taste of violent, impulsive tendencies in juveniles. This would become all too familiar to me later when I was working in Family Court. Paterson was a decaying mill town, rough around the edges and rough in the middle too. The students were a mix of white, Hispanic, and Black. The one thing they had in common was that they all came from poverty-stricken backgrounds.

Most of the teachers in Paterson Public School 8 had basically resigned themselves to the idea that this was just a job and these kids were not going to be educated. The administration occasionally brought in substitute teachers who wouldn't last a day in the tumultuous school environment. One time, I left my classroom for all of two minutes and returned to find one of the students had been knocked out cold.

I have to say I surprised myself. I enjoyed the experience. I met a lot of memorable characters. The principal was definitely not the right guy for a place with an atmosphere like P.S. 8. One day, I heard a squawk from the intercom in my classroom, and it was the principal.

"I have just apprehended one of your students," his disembodied voice informed me. "I found him tap dancing and doing other un-American activities on the stage in the auditorium. I'm giving him twenty lashes with a wet noodle and sending him back to your classroom."

Discipline was hit and miss. In a nod to their deprived home environments, the students all received a daily ration of milk. A kid named Fernando used to come to class with snacks his first-generation immigrant mother baked. Fernando called one snack "squirrel nut cookies," while another was a smelly kind of onion cookie. He'd eat the onion-flavored one and then run around the classroom breathing into the faces of his classmates, grossing them out.

"Fernando, you can't do that," I told him.

"You're not my mother," he sassed back. "You don't get to tell me what to do."

He wouldn't quit. Day after day at milk time, it was the same routine. Finally one day, as he dashed around breathing onion fire, I had had enough.

"That's it, my friend," I announced. "You're going to the principal's office."

I opened the door to usher him out of class. He leaped up from his seat, ran to the back of the room, opened the window, and jumped out. It was a ten-foot drop to the ground. The whole class, me included, rushed to the window and watched the little kid scurrying away into the distance.

That was it for Fernando. P.S. 8 never saw him again.

Around that time, and without really realizing it, I began another phase of my education, just as vital as anything I ever learned in class. I met my future wife, Shelley, on August 15, 1970.

On that day, I went on an outing with a friend of mine to Orchard Beach, the "Riviera of the Bronx." We encountered a group of people he knew. Among them was young Shelley Melamed, who sat in the sand doing a crossword puzzle. I wanted to help her out with the clues, but I was comically bad at crosswords. She was very good, and we both had a laugh at my ineptitude.

Shelley came from a similar background to mine. She grew up in the Bronx in a lower middle-class family. Her parents, like mine, didn't drive. Unlike me, she was an excellent student and graduated at the top of her class in high school and City College. After she graduated from college, Shelley and I got married in November 1972. She was twenty-one and I was twenty-five. She became a secondary school math teacher and eventually became the Upper School Director at a private school. I was smart enough to marry a woman much brighter than me who kept me grounded and provided wise counsel.

Shelley would also be the key to raising our two wonderful children, Jill, born in 1978, and David, born in 1983. They inherited her smarts and my ability to deal with people. She was the disciplinarian who kept them in line. I never raised a finger to my kids or rarely my voice, for that matter. All I had to do was look at them and tell them that I was disappointed in them when they did something wrong. It would immediately bring my daughter to tears, causing them both to feel as if they had committed a capital crime.

I jokingly tell people that Shelley came to my rescue when we first met, that she'd saved me from bullies who were kicking sand in my face at Orchard Beach. We starting dating in the fall of 1970, about the same time that I began night classes at Brooklyn Law School.

CHAPTER 3

MY LIFE IN CRIME

S ometimes I jokingly refer to my professional experience as "my life in crime." I did not develop my perceptions in the airless confines of a think tank. I'll take you into "the rooms where it happens"—the inner sanctums where decisions are made, where policy becomes practice, where the twin values of public safety and justice get thrashed out in the real world.

I received my education as a prosecutor by way of the courtrooms of 100 Centre Street in New York City. Even if you might not be aware of it, you've seen this building. Featured in countless movies and television shows, the New York County Criminal Court at 100 Centre stands as an enduring symbol of the justice system in America.

Built in the late 1930s by the Public Works Administration of FDR's New Deal, the seventeen-story courthouse served as my home away from home for almost a quarter century. I have a great fondness for the structure with its Art Deco architectural touches.

The courthouse rises amid a thicket of other grand government edifices in the neighborhood known as the Civic Center. The buildings located in this area accommodate the Federal District Court, the New York Supreme Court (Civil Term), and such additional adjuncts as Family Court and Surrogate's Court. If the justice system glowed, this little section of Manhattan real estate would be visible from space.

History haunts the neighborhood as well. Across the street

from 100 Centre is Collect Pond Park, the name of which commemorates the original body of water on the site, a spring-fed lake used by the Lenape tribe and the Dutch colonists of New Amsterdam. Down Lafayette Street is the Tweed Courthouse, built by the corrupt administration of Boss Tweed, the chieftain of the Tammany Hall political machine.

The area's narrow, busy streets feature countless shops and eateries that cater to the cops, clerks, lawyers, judges, and other staffers who work in the courts. Nearby Columbus Park hosted the DA's softball league, where I played second base on the Special Narcotics Prosecutor's team that won the championship for four straight years.

A little farther afield is Little Italy and the city's dense Chinatown neighborhood, with its restaurants, fish markets, and funeral parlors. The Brooklyn Bridge, once up for sale to the gullible, feeds a constant flow of bicycles, pedestrians, and vehicle traffic back and forth across the East River.

This was the "Centre of the world," so to speak, my turf, my stomping ground, the place where I drew my lines in the sand and fought my battles. This is where "my life in crime" started.

In the spring of 1973, I was finishing my next to last year at Brooklyn Law School, which was located in downtown Brooklyn around the corner from Borough Hall. A classmate of mine casually mentioned an employment opportunity at the district attorney's office across the bridge in Manhattan.

"You know they're hiring interns over there," he said. "Paralegals."

"Really? At the Manhattan DA?" The potential job opening "over there" was news to me. "You know, that'd be interesting."

My classmate nodded. "The word came through that they're looking to fill positions, and they're taking applications from law school students."

The physical distance from downtown Brooklyn to downtown Manhattan, from Borough Hall to the Municipal Building, measured almost exactly a mile, but it might just as well have been calculated in light-years. For many people at that time, Manhattan represented the center of the world. Brooklyn, Queens, the Bronx, and Staten Island were considered the outer boroughs. In a quirk of local speech, residents of the other boroughs would say, "I'm going into the city," whenever they spoke of heading into Manhattan. This was common usage even though folks from the other boroughs also lived in "the city."[1]

Growing up in the Bronx, I expressed myself exactly that way. "We're heading into the city," I'd tell my childhood friends, which we didn't do all that often.

The prospect of working in the important office of the Manhattan District Attorney was enticing, no matter what the position. I learned that the job's formal title was not intern, not paralegal, but "trial preparation assistant," which sounded a little grander and more serious. At the time, I was making $8,000 a year teaching in the Bronx while going to law school in Brooklyn at night. The trial preparation assistant (TPA) job paid around $7,800.

The difference in pay was negligible, but as a newly married couple just starting out, just scraping by, every penny counted. The deciding factor was that the job offered me entry into a career that fascinated me.

The court system divides itself into two realms. Civil actions involve one party suing another, seeking redress for harm. On the

---

1 In other parts of the United States, boroughs are called "counties," or in certain areas in the South, "parishes." However, each of the five boroughs of New York City is a county of New York State. Manhattan is New York County, Brooklyn is King's County, and Staten Island is Richmond County, alongside Queens County and Bronx County.

other hand, the criminal courts deal with individuals violating the rules contained in the penal law, directives that protect public safety and direct, shape, and limit individual actions. Simply put: it's the world of people behaving badly and getting caught.

I had always had an interest in the nitty-gritty side of the legal world. The extremes of human behavior always fascinated me. I was drawn to books, TV shows, and movies depicting crime and punishment. I'm a crime buff, with a lifelong interest in that area.

I applied by letter for the TPA job and was called in for an interview at what was then 155 Leonard Street in Lower Manhattan. The District Attorney then was a legendary figure named Frank Hogan (so legendary, in fact, that 155 Leonard Street was renamed One Hogan Place after he died). Connecticut born, Columbia University educated, Hogan had already been in office for over three decades when I showed up with my hat in hand, a humble job applicant for a paralegal position.

I was interviewed by Joan C. Sudolnik, a tall, thin, hard-working, chain-smoking dynamo with short brown hair. Then serving as an Assistant District Attorney in the Supreme Court Bureau, Sudolnik later went on to become a New York County Supreme Court Justice. The interview went well, and she offered me the position, which I quickly accepted.

I knew her boss, Frank Hogan, mainly by reputation, an old-school guy whose golden rule was civility. If anyone in his office got a call from an attorney, they had damn well better return that call. Hogan upheld a simple motto, emblazoned on all of his campaign posters: "Don't play politics with people's lives." His tenure at DANY (District Attorney New York) went back to Thomas Dewey's time as a celebrated racket-busting district attorney who later became the governor of New York. Dewey is best remembered now as a popular "almost" president. Some might recall the erroneous 1948 headline, "Dewey Defeats Truman."

As a DA, Frank Hogan followed in Dewey's footsteps and took down a few prominent gangsters himself, including the corrupt Fulton Fish Market kingpin Joe "Socks" Lanza, pretty-boy killer Joe Adonis, and gambler Frank Erickson, right-hand man to famed oddsmaker Arnold Rothstein. The office prosecuted *The $64,000 Question* scandals that were featured in the 1994 film *Quiz Show*, went after government corruption, and targeted comedian Lenny Bruce with obscenity charges.

By 1973, when I joined the DA's office, Hogan was aging and sick. In the midst of swirling allegations that Hogan had been soft on corruption, a Kennedy-family protégé named William Jacobus Vanden Heuvel challenged Hogan in the primary election for NY District Attorney. In Democratic New York City, the primary is usually the whole ball game.

Vanden Heuvel had a lot of weight behind him. He served under CIA founding father William "Wild Bill" Donovan in the Thai embassy during the run-up to the Vietnam War, and was involved in various power positions in New York State politics. Nevertheless, Hogan won the election for district attorney one last time. I never would have much personal interaction with Hogan, but he left an indelible mark on the office, shaping it for years to come.

Hogan headed up the Manhattan District Attorney's office with multiple layers of bureaucracy beneath him. He functioned as the CEO and rarely appeared in court to argue a case himself, but instead orchestrated the thousands of cases that flowed through the office. He had numerous executives assisting him. The most important staffers for the smooth dispensing of justice were the cadre of assistant district attorneys, the ADAs. When I joined as a trial prep assistant, there were around one hundred fifty ADAs in the district attorney's office compared to over five hundred today.

The ADA is the workhorse of the justice system. Assistant

district attorneys—often referred to as "assistants"—prepare the cases, present them to the grand jury, work out plea bargains, deal with judges, and ultimately take the case to trial if it is not disposed of by defendants admitting their guilt. The Manhattan District Attorney—and it has always been a "him," as a woman has never held the job at the time of this writing—represents the public face of the office. He is responsible for setting the tone, establishing overall policies and procedures, and making hiring and firing decisions, but he doesn't really get involved in the day-to-day operations of the office. If you want to really understand the justice system, speak to an ADA.

The year I toiled as a trial preparation assistant proved invaluable. I was pretty much at the bottom of the totem pole in the DA's office. When I started out, I was like the Greek philosopher Socrates, in that the only thing I knew was that I knew nothing. I was assigned to work alongside three ADAs in the Supreme Court Bureau. As far as I could tell, the assignment was random, as if the powers that be merely pulled three names out of a hat. At that time, there were a few dozen assistants who worked out of the offices of the New York County Supreme Court Bureau at 100 Centre. I learned the basics of scheduling court dates, assembling evidence, preparing witnesses, and keeping track of the voluminous amounts of paperwork that the justice system generated. In the process, almost without realizing it, I learned the ins and outs of how the office operated. The three ADAs were Jack Frost, Mike Nadel, and Mark A. Meyer.

I would have to say Frost lived up to his name somewhat, with a slight chilliness to his personality. He was soft-spoken, quiet, and slightly aloof. He wasn't someone you'd get personally close to, but he was professional in all the right ways. He went on to hold the position of Trial Bureau Chief in the office.

Mike Nadel did not make use of me all that much. He later

became a criminal court judge and an executive in the Brooklyn District Attorney's Office.

I had actually known Mark A. Meyer while in school at Fairleigh Dickinson University—knew him, as in we would say "hello" in passing. He was an expert on getting things done and was a big man on campus, which I most definitely was not. We became close associates and good friends during our time working together.

I learned by watching Meyer in action. He was the warmest of the three ADAs to whom I was assigned. He had a great sense of humor and laughed a lot, a real schmoozer who could joke with the judges. Though he was extremely successful there, Meyer eventually proved too restless to stay in the DA's office for long. He moved on to private practice, where he played an instrumental role in opening Romania to the West and creating the new nation of Moldova.

The bureau system helped organize the thousands of cases that came into DANY. The major bureaus were the Criminal Courts Bureau, the Indictment Bureau, and the Supreme Court Bureau. Other specialized bureaus included Appeals, Rackets, Frauds, and the Homicide Bureau. Cases were classified as either misdemeanors or felonies and then transferred to the appropriate bureau.

I worked on cases dealing with street crimes such as robbery, burglary, assault, and rape, where the arrests were made by beat cops and detectives. The trial preparation I did for the ADAs might have been routine, but I found it interesting, even compelling. Each case had a folder, or "case jacket," which contained a copy of the criminal court papers and the indictment.

My job was to organize, expand, and fill in the case jacket so the file contained everything an ADA would possibly need for trial. I would obtain the defendant's criminal record, subpoena the police records on the case, including the UF61, which was the criminal complaint report prepared by a police officer, and the DD5 reports, which were written by detectives. Another crucial document included in the case jacket file was the grand jury minutes. During a grand jury proceeding, the ADA presented evidence that there was probable cause to believe that the defendant committed the crime. This established a loose framework that the ADA in the subsequent criminal trial could use to obtain a conviction.

Sometimes, arresting officers would come in for interviews, especially on cases that the ADA thought would go to trial, as opposed to those being plea-bargained out. I needed to nail down the facts the arresting officers would testify about. I also occasionally interviewed complainants, who were the victims of the crime in question.

It was important that the facts were accurate so a defense attorney couldn't exploit the testimony or evidence in any way, such as impeaching a police officer, challenging a complainant, or disputing the prosecutor's version of events. "No surprises in court" should have been tattooed on every trial preparation assistant's forehead, a guiding principle emphasized again and again by every ADA.

Felony trials are the closest we get in the legal world to gladiator arenas, where lives and futures hang in the balance. It's absolutely imperative to dot every *i* and cross every *t*. If Frost, Nadel, or Meyer ever got caught flat-footed in court, or if a complainant hadn't been prepared properly to testify, or if the testimony of a witness strayed from the expected, it could severely hurt the case and lead directly to the acquittal of a guilty person.

After my year as a TPA, I hoped to take the next step up and be accepted as an assistant district attorney at DANY. My career as an ADA started with a bizarre twist, when I was hired, fired, and re-hired almost within a month.

In 1973 I was in the last year of law school attending classes at night. The previous year of getting my feet wet as a TPA had served me very well. I knew the office and the office knew me. I had a leg up during the interview process, with recommendations from all the ADAs I had worked under. It was essential that I had their backing, as well as getting good recommendations from the other ADAs who had interviewed me.

So it was logical that DA Frank Hogan would hire me as an assistant district attorney. Until I passed the bar exam and was admitted as an attorney, my involvement in trials was limited to misdemeanors, not the serious stuff like felonies.

That was the plan, anyway, but as they say, mankind makes plans and God laughs. Frank Hogan became increasingly sick and had to resign the DA's position (he died a few months later). Malcom Wilson, the governor of New York at the time, appointed Richard Kuh, a former assistant district attorney who worked under Hogan, as the interim district attorney until a special election could be held in November 1974.

The new DA threw a wrench into the works. "I will not be obliged to accept any of my predecessor's prior staff selections," Kuh announced. Then he rescinded my appointment along with every other new hire.

I think the move was Kuh's way of asserting himself, declaring his independence from his former boss, and proving to the world that he was his own man. Kuh had previously worked as Hogan's Chief of the Criminal Courts Bureau and was one of his most trusted aides. Under Hogan's direction, it was Kuh who had obtained the guilty verdict in the obscenity trial of Lenny Bruce.

He was Phi Beta Kappa at Columbia and earned his law degree at Harvard Law. Great credentials, indeed, but Kuh was no Frank Hogan. Holding office for over three decades, Hogan had been a towering figure in New York legal circles.

None of this logic—or illogic—mattered to me. To mix metaphors a bit, just when I had gotten my foot in the door, I had been kicked to the curb. I was hired and let go with such alacrity that my head was spinning. I didn't know what my status was. After I received Hogan's offer of employment, I had stopped interviewing for other jobs because I thought my future was secure. Now I was in limbo.

I loved DANY and felt I was a good fit for it. Would I have to go into private practice? Join a law firm where everyone was engaged in a frantic battle to make partner? The prospect did not appeal to me in the least. Neither did the fallback idea of going back to teaching.

After a few confused days I received a curt notice that interim-DA Kuh would interview several law students who had been given positions by Hogan, the very people who had just been booted off the job. I was among the chosen few. Kuh re-interviewed me and again hired me on as an assistant district attorney.

I aspired to be like my role models: Jack Frost, Mike Nadel, and Mark Meyer. The Manhattan DA's office was where names were made, the most exciting, most important, most prestigious local jurisdiction in the land. Some of the brightest legal minds in the city and country passed through that office. Numerous federal and state judges were DANY alumni, as well as some of the top defense attorneys and litigators in the country. Prominent public officials who have emerged from DANY include Secretary of State William Rogers and Supreme Court Justice Sonia Sotomayor.

As a TPA, I had been going about my main job of helping my three assistants, completing case files and interviewing officers of the NYPD. But I also had accomplished a collateral secondary purpose, one that would prove vital to my future. It's a time-honored aspect of the intern's job to meet people, see and be seen, become a familiar face. *Oh, he belongs here,* this or that judge or lawyer would think, seeing me in courtrooms or around the various offices.

I learned everyone's names. I came to understand the labyrinthine layout of 100 Centre. I officially entered a profession that would become my passion.

CHAPTER 4

COPS AND ROBBERS

Not everything I saw during those early days appeared clear to me. Not everything split neatly along the lines of good guys versus bad guys. Shades of gray arose, in contrast to the black-and-white world of TV crime dramas. I encountered situations that made me question my role within the vast apparatus of the criminal justice system.

Working with officers of the New York City Police Department for the first time opened my eyes to street-level realities and real-world moral compromises. Before that, I might have had innocuous interactions with cops while growing up in the Bronx, or in the course of working as a schoolteacher in Paterson, New Jersey, and in New York City. None of these encounters were serious. I had never been arrested. I spent my entire life in the New York metropolitan area and had managed to emerge totally clean as far as the criminal justice system was concerned.

In August 1974, I officially began my career as an assistant district attorney. When I worked as a TPA, I was thrown into the criminal justice system. I'd spent my days interacting with police, helping them file their reports, serving as an interface between them and the assistant prosecutors in the office. They were beat cops—a few of them were detectives, but generally they came in straight off the street.

I was assigned to the Criminal Courts Bureau, where most of

the new assistants were placed. There were twenty-five rookie assistants who were given office space on the ninth floor in the quarters we called "blue heaven" because of the color of the walls. In the Criminal Court Bureau, we handled misdemeanor cases, as well as the calendars for the criminal and arraignment parts.

I served as one of the steps in a filtering process that the district attorney's office used to assess the criminal complaints that the NYPD brought in. We judged each arrest on whether it qualified as a legally sufficient case, and, if so, it was classified as a felony or misdemeanor.

Here's how the process worked: An arrest would come into the complaint room and an assistant district attorney would write up the applicable charges. If it was a misdemeanor case, the file would get a blue back cover, while a felony would be yellow. The next step would be the arraignment, which would be handled in one of two courts: AR-1 (Arraignment Part 1) or AR-2 (Arraignment Part 2). The assistant district attorney would review the complaint and the criminal record of the accused.

Various actions could be taken. A misdemeanor might lead to an offer of a plea deal. A felony could be reduced to a misdemeanor if the offense was not serious and be pleaded out. The ADA could also make a request for bail depending on the severity of the crime and the possibility of a flight risk.

If no plea was taken, the case would continue its journey through the system, moving on to a criminal court part. Those parts were labeled in an odd, non-consecutive manner, as AP 1, AP 3, AP 5, AP 7, AP 9, and AP 17—the designation AP standing for "All Purpose." For serious felonies, the case would be sent to the Indictment Bureau and presented to a grand jury.

If the grand jury voted to indict, the case would be sent up to the New York County Supreme Court. The clerks would give the case an indictment number (e.g., 1423 of 2023) and forward it to be placed on the calendar of a specific judge. The case would then be prosecuted by an ADA in the Supreme Court Bureau.

The calendar judge would handle any motions made by the parties and try to work out a plea bargain. If the case couldn't be disposed of this way, it would be sent to another judge for hearings and trial. In the end, the vast majority of cases never got to trial. They either ended up with the defendant pleading guilty, or the case being dismissed because either the witnesses failed to appear in court, or evidence was tainted by improper police conduct, such as an illegal search.

This was assembly line justice, with different ADAs handling different elements of the process. It was like a car factory worker in Detroit, who might be dedicated all day long to a specific task, installing steering wheels or windshields. At 100 Centre, the arrangement involved multiple ADAs and tended to result in a disjointed, myopic approach to each case. The system was ripe for the kind of reform that would soon come.

Day in and day out, NYPD officers trooped into DANY, pouring forth accounts of crimes, both misdemeanors and, less often, felonies. Each report represented a story of sorts, a short, punchy narrative from the mean streets of New York City. Domestic incidents, sale and possession of narcotics, murder, rape, robbery, assault, burglary, and grand larceny auto were just some of the crimes the police dealt with every day. It felt as though the cops had sliced open the bulging underbelly of the city and everything sick, nasty, and bad spilled out.

That period of my life served as a wake-up call for a straight arrow, somewhat sheltered kid from the Bronx. The experience drove home a fundamental truth: *everyone* in the world, no matter their race, ethnic background, religion, gender, or sexual orientation, wants to be safe in their homes, on the streets, and in their neighborhoods. Safety is and should be a guiding principle of the justice system. In fact, perhaps the justice system should be renamed the *safety system*, as the idea of security is so crucial and fundamental to the average citizen.

I later learned that the protection of our citizens is sometimes taken for granted during periods of historically low crime rates. Safety is somehow not appealing enough to rally around, not cool, not sexy. The idea of justice, or rather injustice, seems to be the kind of cause that can get protestors out onto the streets.

Here's a situation that everyone in the system notices straight off. It can be stated as a syllogism: "Justice is dispensed by human beings, human beings are flawed, therefore the justice system is flawed." This represents an obvious rule of thumb.

Looking back, I was incredibly green. Like many people new to the job, I tended to see situations in simple terms. Psychologists call it "splitting," where things are seen in black and white. I accepted almost everything any cop told me without question. I took the statements made in their incident reports as gospel.

I would come to understand that this is a common character-istic of newbies. Newcomers on the prosecutorial side of things tend to be believers, either because it's simpler that way, or because they have to support the police, don't they? Newcomers on the defense side of the courtroom tend to trust what the defendant tells them, chapter and verse, invariably believing their client to be innocent or the object of wrongful police conduct. Oftentimes, they will proclaim their client's innocence even when he has been caught red-handed.

As I gained experience, I realized reality wasn't exactly black and white. With practice and experience, the right angles got knocked off my rigid viewpoint. After processing the thousandth police arrest report and encountering the same style of police testimony over and over again, I became a little less of a babe in the woods.

Did I encounter bias and racism among the police officers I interviewed and worked with? Did I hear the n-word, the characterizations of street criminals as "mutts," "skells," "animals," and "dirtbags"? Yes. Am I shocked, *shocked*, that such attitudes persist? Not so much, not after years in the prosecutor's office. But as a new, inexperienced ADA, I found such offensiveness to be eye-opening.

The racism issues I encountered usually involved street-level cops on the beat rather than the higher-ups. One problem was that a lot of these cops came from the suburbs. Where did NYPD officers tend to live? Not in Manhattan. The rent was too high, for one thing, and birds of a feather tend to flock together. At least half the officers I encountered lived in specific places like Long Island, Westchester, Staten Island, or the northern suburbs for those who didn't mind a longer commute.

Most of the officers I met were white cops who came out of suburban environments. They were thrown into minority neighborhoods and were dealing with people they had very, very little experience with. They didn't understand the local culture. Everything they heard was that the folks they were policing were "bad" people who were up to no good and had to be taken off the street.

Cultural sensitivity training in the NYPD? Not when I started out in the 1970s. Diversity? It was, by and large, a white male police force. The DA's office was also overwhelmingly white and male, too, but effectively served as something of a corrective to the prejudiced attitudes of some of the beat cops. I know the vast majority of the people who live in urban communities are hardworking, law-abiding citizens. They want to live a normal life. They want to be safe. They also want to be able to take a walk in their own neighborhoods without being hassled, and that includes being tossed up against the wall by police.

Frank Hogan preached that every case should be based on the facts and the evidence, period. Race should not factor in as an issue. The main goal of a district attorney, as I learned from Hogan and later from his eventual successor in the office, Robert Morgenthau, is to seek justice. In other words, the role of the district attorney is to prosecute the guilty while also ensuring the innocent are not prosecuted for crimes they didn't commit, crimes that cannot be proven, or crimes tainted by ill-gotten evidence or by improperly taken statements. If someone is prosecuted, make certain they're prosecuted fairly and sentenced fairly and consistently, regardless of skin color. Justice should be colorblind.

In truth, the role of the prosecutor's office is limited. It's a very specific slice of the justice system pie. Prosecutors are not social workers. We aren't responsible for ameliorating the defendants' home environment, their mental health, or their economic status.

As a society, we might forget the limits of a prosecutor's responsibilities. A district attorney is not God, though I've seen a few DAs who might question that assumption. The public desires justice that is perfect, immune to being swayed by outside considerations, a paragon of probity. But, of course, nothing human can be perfect.

Even being aware of the boundaries of a DA's function, the office always operates with limited resources. DAs are always fighting for money. How they choose to spend that money is vital to the dispensation of justice. Should a district attorney's office spend money on people who have been convicted and sent to jail, as some of the new progressive politicians have demanded? In those situations, our job has already ended. We have to go on to the next case and make sure it is being handled correctly.

Can prosecutors take steps to try to lessen the number of people who are incarcerated? Absolutely. Can they limit the kind of convictions that are going to impact the accused for the rest of their lives? Yes. But the bottom line is that prosecutors have to deal with those people who've committed crimes, especially violent crimes, and make sure those crimes are adjudicated, that the guilty are prosecuted, and that justice has been served.

Hard truths became real to me during my first exposure to the high-powered world of the Manhattan DA's office. I learned that the goals of justice and public safety required a balancing act. I eventually accepted the obvious fact that while police officers work within the supposedly blind justice system, some are nonetheless loaded with wide-ranging personal opinions, individual biases, and heavy-duty emotional baggage. Some cops had agendas of their own.

Judging from the pronouncements of politicians I encountered, and the opinions put forth by the supposedly wise souls in the media, I'm not sure the public is aware of these truths. Yes, we want a perfect justice system. But again, as in any system that involves human beings, perfection is a goal toward which to work, not a reality to maintain.

During the Hogan and Morgenthau years I believe the New York County District Attorney's Office was among the best in the world. Its sterling reputation certainly indicates that. When I worked there, I knew it for its faults, but I also knew it for its considerable achievements.

I knew it as an office where the ADAs were dedicated to seeing justice done, where ADAs weren't judged on their conviction rates or on how many defendants they sent to jail. Promotions were based on merit. Some ADAs were excellent trial lawyers, while others were superb investigators who could untangle complex fraud or organized crime schemes. Other ADAs were great at writing appellate briefs and arguing cases on appeal.

Throughout my entire time at the DA's office, I never encountered a hint of corruption, bribery, or an unlawful act among the ADAs. Of course, there were instances when an ADA screwed up. We are only human, after all. When you handle the volume of cases that ADAs work on, mistakes are inevitably going to be made. Some assistants made bad judgment calls, such as not following a judge's directive, or failing to turn over exculpatory evidence, or not closely scrutinizing the evidence and testimony of witnesses. But overwhelmingly, ADAs try to do the right thing, doing their utmost best to ensure that innocent people are not convicted of crimes they did not commit.

Why do people seek to become prosecutors? Because they want to serve the public, make the streets safer for residents, and improve people's lives. There are other attractions, such as the excitement, intensity, and importance of the work. For me, and for the overwhelming majority of my colleagues, the answer to "why be a prosecutor?" was simply the desire to do good.

Why did DANY rise to the top? To me, the answer seemed obvious, and involved the high quality of leadership. During his long tenure in office, Frank Hogan established a rigorous standard of professionalism. But beyond Hogan, I came to attribute a large part of our success to the determined efforts, incorruptible character, and strong-willed personality of one of the most influential and respected individuals I have ever met.

Robert Morgenthau.

CHAPTER 5

CRIMINAL COURT

Although he would outlast me by a decade, Robert Morris Morgenthau and I assumed our respective positions in the Manhattan DA's office almost at the same time—he, in 1975, via a special election to the top job, me, in 1974, by getting hired as an assistant district attorney. More than anyone else of that period, Morgenthau would shape the legal system of New York City and its public policies.

Morgenthau had a great influence on my professional life. Like almost all my co-workers, I would come to refer to him with the simple, single-word moniker of "Boss." In many ways, I saw him as a model and a symbol of what a public prosecutor should be. For intelligence, political savvy, and effectiveness, I can't think of anyone who equaled him.

Robert Morgenthau grew up in Manhattan and at a country manor in the Hudson Valley. His grandfather made millions in real estate and became the ambassador to Turkey. His mother's uncle founded the Wall Street investment firm, Lehman Brothers. His father served as the Treasury Secretary in the administration of a nearby country neighbor of the family, President Franklin Delano Roosevelt.

Traveling in such rarified, well-connected circles, Morgenthau attended prep schools and earned degrees at Amherst and Yale Law. From an early age, he knew everybody who was anybody, including John F. Kennedy. Like JFK, he was a genuine U.S. Navy hero in World War II, serving on destroyers in both the European and Pacific theaters. Two of the ships that he served on were sunk under him, and one was attacked by a kamikaze pilot. Due to his time in combat, he lost a substantial part of his hearing in one ear.

He later spoke about a promise he'd made to the Almighty during the sinking of the first ship. As he struggled to stay afloat without a lifejacket alongside his shipwrecked comrades in the night-time waters of the Mediterranean, he proposed a deal with God. *Get me through this alive,* he offered, *and I promise I will try to do something useful with my life.* He survived and dedicated himself to making good on that promise.

In the 1960s, Morgenthau climbed aboard the Kennedy bandwagon and rode it to an appointment as the U.S. Attorney for the Southern District of New York. He ran for governor twice, failing both times. It took him a while to find his true public calling, which was service as the Manhattan District Attorney.

Here was the well-pedigreed figure who commanded DANY for almost my entire time there. Meanwhile, I was a Bronx boy who came from a family barely clinging to its lower middle-class status. Morgenthau often wore an ancient cardigan with holes in it, a garment anyone with an impoverished background would not be caught dead in. *The New York Times* labeled him "Gotham's aristocratic Mr. District Attorney."

Even with his impressive family background, Morgenthau had a streak of New York City street smarts in his character. An outstanding quality about him was his unerring judgment. He was persistent in the extreme, a bulldog, a very shrewd guy who knew how to get things done.

Morgenthau also had the last word about which ADAs would work for him. The Manhattan DA's office received more resumes than any other local prosecutor in the country. The resumes went through a screening process that winnowed them down to a few dozen or so candidates. The Boss played no part in the process until his Director of Legal Hiring forwarded the finalists to him. Morgenthau would interview them and decide who made the final cut.

In January 1975, I passed the bar and was formally admitted to the legal profession, the same month Morgenthau took office. Upon admission, my salary went from $11,500 to $13,000 a year, which would be about $74,000 today. I considered myself a rich guy.

All assistant district attorneys took their places within the various bureaus of the office, assigned here or there according to a seemingly random logic. I was too inexperienced to rank the various positions in terms of prestige, though from my time as an intern, I knew that if any of my fellow ADAs were assigned to the Appeals Bureau, somebody upstairs must have thought they were smart, talented writers.

Most of the new hires, including me, went to the Criminal Court Bureau, where we dealt mostly with run-of-the-mill misdemeanors. The first case I ever tried concerned a jostling charge, which was the legal term for pickpocketing.

A couple of other new ADAs were assigned to the Complaint Bureau. This should not be confused with the Complaint Room, which was where the write-up of charges first took place. ADAs in the Complaint Bureau dealt directly with ordinary citizens registering grievances and reporting crimes, real or imagined. Some of the citizen complaints were legitimate. But this being New York City, a few were too odd to be believed.

"I'm being followed by Martians," Mr. John Q. Public might say. "The tinfoil on my antennae gives them away." Other complaints consisted of people stating that their apartments were bugged or that someone was controlling their brains. The exasperated ADAs writing up reports in the Complaint Bureau were always good for a story or two.

The Criminal Court Bureau exposed me to a share of oddities as well, but mostly I witnessed a seemingly endless parade of misery and bad behavior. I felt as though I was really seeing the city for the first time. During those first few months in criminal court, it was as if I had become fully awakened to urban realities.

The criminal court calendars handled well over a hundred cases a day. Paraded before the court were an endless march of prostitutes, car thieves, robbers, rapists, burglars, drunken drivers, fare beaters, and murderers. Any crime you can think of would end up on the criminal court docket. Judges and prosecutors worked long days to handle this ever-present flow of cases.

I saw what was really happening on the streets. I was exposed to a crime-ridden city, dealing with everything from the least serious type of misconduct to the most serious. When I added it all together, I got a sense of the utter relentlessness of crime. The chaos never seemed to let up. Thanksgiving, Christmas, Memorial Day, Fourth of July . . . the time of year didn't matter. It's hard for anyone to grasp just how much crime is out there.

The experience matured me. At times, I felt like the proverbial sacrificial lamb, chosen to absorb the impact of society's evil. I saw the terrible toll crime and violence took on people's lives. Unless they experience it directly, people can't get the full picture of what's going on.

The cops knew. They arrested people they considered lower than low. "Skells" was the favored term the NYPD used to describe the decrepit characters it came up against. Street cops especially found it hard to have compassion when they constantly encountered violent, crazed, or deviant behavior. The crimes seemed out of proportion to what was gained from them.

Day by day, I processed cases involving fare beaters, pick-pockets, stick-up guys, and kids who stole cars. Many of the incidents made no sense to me. Two friends are sitting on a stoop drinking beer together when suddenly they get into an argument and one guy stomps the other guy's face in. Two young men get into a fight in a bar and engage in a fistfight, and one guy falls, hits his head, and dies. A young kid who is an addict steals money from his parents and they have him arrested because they can't control him anymore.

Some cases would tug at me emotionally. Eventually, I reacted with less and less shock to the incredible kind of behaviors people engaged in. Very little surprised me anymore. I gradually built up a detached attitude toward wrongdoing. As I became more deeply aware of the state of things, I taught myself to be dispassionate when evaluating situations and crimes. I learned to handle cases efficiently, to judge relative levels of lawbreaking. At the beginning, every assault on the rule of law seemed deadly serious. As I processed more cases, I differentiated which ones deserved the most attention.

Discovering a purpose in my job saved me from cynicism. I saw my role as beating back the chaos in the streets as best I could, attempting to establish some degree of order in an environment that at times seemed to have gone totally off the rails. I realized I couldn't solve every problem, but I was determined to do the best I could.

During the year I spent in the Criminal Court Bureau, I accumulated a tremendous amount of experience writing complaints, working with police officers, processing arraignments, and trying cases. At that point I knew I was probably in line for an appointment to the Indictment Bureau or headed into the Supreme Court Bureau, which handled the most serious felonies outside of the Homicide Bureau. I felt prepared for the next step.

From the beginning, I learned a lot from Robert Morgenthau. He had an immense amount of power, but he knew better than to show it. He was never flashy. His authority wasn't so much for public display but rather in the minds and opinions of others. People would tread carefully around him because they knew his reach, his abilities, and his influence. A lot of what he accomplished was done behind closed doors. That was where he exercised his power.

Morgenthau understood the need for adequate resources to run the office efficiently. Part of the reason for his longevity in office was his political acumen, integrity, and persistence. But part of it was also his skill at obtaining ample funding for the DA's office. In 1975, at the start of his term, the annual budget registered at a measly $8 million, a sum that actually ran out halfway through the fiscal year. By the time Morgenthau retired three-and-a-half decades later, the office had a staff of over five hundred lawyers and a $125 million annual operating budget.

ADAs handle the nuts and bolts business of dispensing justice and can easily make much more than what the government pays if they choose to enter private practice. It's crucial to find funding for salaries that will at least keep assistant district attorneys above the poverty line. In addition, boring, day-to-day, line item overhead is also more important than you might think. A functioning big-city DA's office needs money for surveillance technology, computers, phones, and office supplies.

Idealists believe justice should exist on a lofty plane far above any financial consideration. However, the cold, hard truth is that justice lives and dies in the brutal world of budgetary arithmetic. How many assistant prosecutors can a DA hire? How many investigators are needed? How much equipment and what kind of technology? To carry out justice, you must have a sustainable answer to these questions. Money turns the wheels of justice.

Back when I interned as a TPA, I noticed the Manhattan DA's office seemed a little underfunded and threadbare. The mid-seventies was an era when New York City flirted with bankruptcy. When city administrators went hat in hand to the federal government for a bailout, the then-president's response triggered an infamous tabloid headline: "FORD TO CITY: DROP DEAD!"

Perhaps because of his privileged upbringing, Morgenthau intuitively grasped the intimate relationship between money and justice. He was a realist, not a romantic idealist. His predecessor, Frank Hogan, balanced the annual budget of the DA's office and dutifully returned any surplus to the public coffers. Such an idea would have made Morgenthau shudder. He constantly beat the bushes for federal grant money, forfeiture money, fines . . . money from whatever source he could find.

After examining the budget when he came into office, Morgenthau met with the bureaus separately and made a sobering announcement.

"The city has no money," he told his ADAs. "We can't give you raises. But I've arranged for you to get another week of paid vacation." Added on to the four weeks we had at that time, that fifth week has never been taken back, and is still given to ADAs today.

CHAPTER 6

THE BOSS

The closed doors to DA Morgenthau's office were guarded by an extremely able gatekeeper named Ida Van Lindt. She had served the same function for Frank Hogan, and Morgenthau knew he had to keep her on. You didn't get to see the Boss without going through Ida. She called herself his "office wife." Others called her the "First Lady of DANY."

I admired Morgenthau for making sure he had good people around him, and Ida was definitely one of those. Always well-dressed and well-spoken, with the kind of intelligence that rose to the level of wisdom, she got to know the Boss, what he liked and disliked, his habits, and what was important to him. Crucial to her job, she knew how to handle the numerous calls that came into the office, knowing which ones took priority and which ones to transfer to another office.

"Mr. Morgenthau would like to see you," Ida said on the phone one day, summoning me from my post as an assistant district attorney in the Criminal Court Bureau.

I have to admit I was puzzled upon hearing the summons from the Boss. Mostly I couldn't get over my surprise that the District Attorney of New York County even knew my name. I was one of hundreds of ADAs working on his staff. Why single me out?

I remember taking the elevator to the eighth floor, where the doors opened to reveal a uniformed cop posted as a security measure in front of the entrance to the executive offices. I headed down a long hallway, with the offices of the executive assistants on the left side, and photos of all the prior DAs lining the walls. Through an open door straight ahead sat Ida, the Boss's gatekeeper.

I took my seat on a wooden bench to await my summons. Ida finally waved me through her vestibule into Morgenthau's inner sanctum.

The man was sitting behind a large desk piled over every inch with paper. I've always been one to keep my feet planted solidly on the ground. I didn't tremble in the presence of my superior, wasn't nervous, and didn't say anything foolish. The meeting was just a few minutes face to face. But somewhere underneath the taking care of business, we were sizing each other up.

Morgenthau introduced me to another gentleman present, a writer named Hal Sitowitz, who had written scripts for popular TV shows such as *Gunsmoke* and *The Rookies*. Sitowitz was working on a project that involved the justice system and wanted to be shown around the criminal courts.

I had no idea how or why Morgenthau selected me for the job of tour guide. I never found out if Sitowitz applied any of the lessons he learned during his short time with me. But he sent a letter of thanks and a bottle of cognac.

Carrying the bottle underneath my arm, I went up to the office to report back to Morgenthau. As public servants, we weren't allowed to accept gifts. I told Ida I needed a quick minute with the Boss.

"How'd you do with that guy?" he asked me immediately—no hellos, no small talk, just getting straight to the matter.

"Fine, I guess. He sent a note thanking us."

"Okay!" Morgenthau's tone indicated he considered the matter concluded.

"Boss," I said. "He sent me a bottle of cognac. What am I supposed to do with this? How do I send it back?"

Morgenthau eyed the booze. He wasn't a big drinker. "Don't worry about it," he said. "Just keep it."

He threw his lanky legs up on the edge of the desk and lit one of his beloved Dunhill Montecruz cigars. With the Boss, you always knew when a meeting was over. I trotted out, nodded to Ida, and headed back to my duties.

That was the first of numberless encounters with the man, the first of many Dunhills I watched him smoke, the first of many meetings, both one-on-one and with other staffers present.

I could quote that famous line from the movie *Casablanca*, where Humphrey Bogart says, "I think this is the beginning of a beautiful friendship."

It wasn't that way at all. Morgenthau was too private, too reserved, too removed for friendship. He did not have a magnetic personality, and he didn't do well at press conferences. While he was always extremely well-versed in the issue at hand, he came off as very dry and—not to put too fine a point on it—boring.

Morgenthau ran for governor of New York twice, and both times failed miserably, primarily because he was so stiff out on the campaign trail. He never could master the kind of hail-fellow-well-met bonhomie of an adroit campaigner such as Bill Clinton. Once in a while at campaign events staffers became exasperated to discover their candidate had simply wandered off.

Irving Lang, a State Supreme Court Justice in Manhattan, used to recount a revealing story about Morgenthau's behavior out on the hustings. Morgenthau approached Bayard Rustin, the African American political leader, at a campaign event.

"What are you eating?" asked the always hungry Morgenthau.

"What I'm eating," Rustin replied, "is the reason you lost the election for governor twice." It was a bagel. The meaning behind the remark was that Morgenthau lacked the common touch, the knack of connecting with the local voter no matter where he was, just as Rustin did with his smart choice of street food.

Awkward as he was as a campaigner, Morgenthau still managed to win district attorney elections repeatedly. First of all, he was endorsed by all the newspapers, back when a newspaper endorsement meant something. Second, the success of the office served as the best argument for his re-election.

The office made cases that no other DA made or even tried to make. And because Manhattan was home to national media and bold-face name celebrities, a lot of those cases were very high profile. When you are successfully prosecuting the likes of John Lennon's assassin, subway vigilante Bernard Goetz, or lifestyle doyenne Martha Stewart, it's easy to remind the electorate of what you have accomplished.

Over the course of his career, Morgenthau supervised an incredible total of 3.5 million cases. He stands alone in that respect, and if there is ever a DA's Hall of Fame, he'll be among the first inductees.

After a year in the Criminal Court Bureau, I was promoted to the Supreme Court Bureau, which prosecuted felony crimes. In the fall of 1975, I tried my first felony case, a rape case that took place on the Upper West Side of Manhattan. Over the next few years, as I took on more responsibilities, I gradually got to know the Boss better.

While he could be stiff around voters, Robert Morgenthau was at his best on a more personal level. He and I were friendly, to be sure. He was never frosty and actually had a pretty good sense of humor. He liked to say to me, "Bob, do you have any good jokes and stories for me?" I'd tell him a joke, he'd laugh, and later on I'd hear him repeat the line to others, which made me feel pretty good.

I used to kid with him all the time. Sometimes I would refer to him as the "grand high kabob." In later years, I would perform a friendly mock bow before him, take his hand, and make as if to kiss his ring. He always got a kick out of that. We had a solid rapport.

I broke bread with Morgenthau many times, on the road at legal conferences, and more often at Forlini's. The venerable restaurant on Baxter Street, just across the park from 100 Centre, served as a regular go-to gathering place for everyone in the local legal community. Morgenthau had his own table in the back room. They eventually put up a brass plaque commemorating the spot as his. Sadly, Forlini's closed in March 2022 after seventy-nine years in business. It was the end of an era.

For a thin guy, Morgenthau had a huge appetite. Many times, he would order for himself and then order food for me too.

"This gentleman is hungry," he would say to the waiter. "Can you bring him another salad?" And, of course, he would be the one to eat the salad. His long, bony fingers would reach across the table as he wordlessly retrieved a piece of broccoli or a leftover baked potato from my plate.

In the early eighties, we were in Albany at a retreat dealing with then Governor Mario Cuomo's sentencing guidelines commission. I sat next to Morgenthau, who was soon engaging in his usual tricks of hijacking food from my plate. He ordered a fish dish, while I went with beef with gravy and asparagus. I'm not big on veggies, so after I finished my main dish, there was asparagus and a pool of gravy still on my plate.

There was a group of us at the table, including Joseph Bellacosa, a judge from the New York State Court of Appeals, and two more appellate judges. They watched the District Attorney of Manhattan casually lift the leftover asparagus spears from my plate, eating them one by one. He then tore off pieces of his dinner roll and used them to sop up the gravy. All the while the Boss didn't miss a beat of the conversation.

Toward the end of the meal, the waiter made a move to clear my plate. "Are you finished, sir?" he asked.

"I don't know, I think you better ask him," I said, pointing to Morgenthau. The entire group burst into laughter.

The Boss and I enjoyed an excellent working relationship for over two decades, but there were always firm boundaries. That comic bowing-and-scraping act I performed in front of Morgenthau was clearly supposed to be humorous, but behind the joke lay an element of truth.

I recall a time when Carlo Boccia had just assumed the position of Special Agent in Charge (SAC) of the DEA's New York City office.

"Hey, Bob," Boccia asked me, "could you arrange for me to meet DA Morgenthau? Just an introductory thing—so I can kiss his ring, you know?"

I arranged the meeting, and just before Boccia and I proceeded to lunch at Forlini's, I sounded a cautionary note. "You know how you're here to kiss the man's ring, right, Carlo?"

"Yeah?" he said.

"Well, I hate to tip you off, but Robert Morgenthau keeps his ring in the back pocket of his pants."

Forewarned and forearmed, Boccia went in to meet the Boss.

One of Robert Morgenthau's favorite sayings was "Never trouble trouble until trouble troubles you." Maybe he just liked the wordplay, because the man was, in truth, extremely fond of making trouble, especially when the target was the rich and powerful.

He was smart in that respect, going after financial crime under the theory that anyone who moved vast amounts of money came under the legal jurisdiction of the Manhattan DA. The Federal Reserve Bank was located in the Financial District, at 33 Water Street, just a few blocks away from Morgenthau's headquarters at 100 Centre. The money passed through Manhattan. It went through the Federal Reserve. That's how Morgenthau could make cases pretty much anywhere on the globe. The Fed gave him his "intergalactic" jurisdiction.

He loved corruption cases. For a long time organized crime controlled the carting services in New York City, the private companies that picked up garbage at commercial businesses. This was a problem from way back, a perennial issue that seemed impervious to prosecution. Morgenthau went after the carting industry tooth and nail.

The office also took down several figures involved in corrupt practices in the construction industry. He beefed up the Investigations Division, as well as bureaus that devoted themselves to rackets and frauds. He made cases that took down the big bosses, the corrupt wise guys who were used to having free rein.

"Crime in the suites" mattered to Morgenthau just as much as "crime in the streets." In legal circles he was known as the father of white-collar criminal prosecutions. His assistant prosecutors might prosecute a low-level crook who committed a burglary, but what really made Morgenthau's day was bringing down high-powered figures, corrupt politicians, greedy corporate heads, or organized crime bosses. Those were the cases he relished.

Nobody was too big. Nobody was too high up to avoid justice. Such wrongdoers represented a personal affront to his sense of justice, his commitment to an even-handed application of the law. Morgenthau had been around the wealthy and powerful his entire life. He knew their ways, their attitudes, and their cupidity. He hated the way powerful people assumed they could get away with anything. It offended his moral principles.

His determined search for money to support the office represented another aspect of Morgenthau's "go-after-the-big-fish" policies. He was ingenious when it came to dealing with state politicians in Albany to obtain funding, and urging Washington to create new programs that would be financed with federal support.

Big fish convictions meant big bucks too. Forfeiture money and court costs could be extracted from Wall Street, the coffers of organized crime, or the illicit profits of corrupt businesses. Morgenthau helped pioneer the use of newly passed asset forfeiture legislation to hit criminals where they lived, right in their pocketbooks.

He targeted banks, tax cheats, financial industry swindlers. His successes against corporate crime included taking down Leo Dennis Kozlowski, a former chief executive of Tyco International, a sprawling conglomerate. After two high-profile trials, Kozlowski was sentenced to eight-and-one third to twenty-five years for looting Tyco of $600 million. Fraud charges against Bank of Credit and Commerce International (BCCI) generated $800 million in fines, leading the Bank of England to shutter BCCI in 1991.

These were the kind of cases the Boss lived for, proving his principle that no one was above the law. DANY collected a fortune in seized assets. In 2009, when he finally departed the Manhattan DA's office after thirty-five years, he reportedly left behind a fat going-away present: a half billion dollars in forfeiture money socked away in the public accounts.

One of the few instances where I witnessed Morgenthau raise his voice came in the mid-eighties, at a meeting involving the five city DAs, plus myself as the representative from the Office of Special Narcotics. Even then, because he managed to send me a wry signal mid-battle, it was difficult for me to tell if he was really losing his cool.

We had driven a few blocks away from 100 Centre to the office of the Criminal Justice Coordinator, Peter Benitez, whose thankless job was to try to deal with the various law enforcement entities active in the city. Among the DAs present at the meeting was Elizabeth Holtzman, the Brooklyn District Attorney at the time. Holtzman was a former U.S. congresswoman from New York's 16th District (Chuck Schumer succeeded her in office).

Morgenthau sat at one end of the conference table, while I sat at the other. Out of nowhere, it seemed, Holtzman lobbed a shot over the Boss's bow. "It's clear that the Manhattan office receives a disproportionate amount of funding," she announced. "The imbalance urgently needs to be addressed."

I glanced sideways at Morgenthau. He appeared unruffled and remained sanguine as Holzman launched into a recitation of budget figures and percentages, trying to prove that Morgenthau was getting too big of a slice of the criminal justice pie. Never mind the fact that the Manhattan office made big cases and Morgenthau was an absolute ace when it came to securing money from Albany and Washington.

Midway through Holtzman's spiel, Morgenthau interrupted her. Loudly. He didn't speak, he erupted. It was so out of character, so outlandish, that jaws dropped all around the conference table. He unleashed for a good two or three minutes, screaming and gesticulating. I had never seen anything like it, and no one else in the room had either, as Robert Morgenthau rarely raised his voice. He didn't have to. His words carried enormous weight even if he pronounced them evenly and without the emphasis of volume.

Suddenly, in the midst of his tirade, he looked over at me and winked. As surprising as his overt display of anger was, the wink was more so. I was floored.

The meeting ended with Holtzman's raid effectively beaten back. On our drive back to the office, I felt I had to ask.

"Boss," I said. "What was that all about? One minute you're shouting at her, and the next minute you're winking at me!"

Morgenthau gave a hoarse laugh. "Sometimes a little righteous indignation goes a long way."

From that point forward, it seemed to me Liz Holtzman avoided confronting Morgenthau. I didn't blame her. As I said, I enjoyed a fine relationship with the Boss. We got along famously, and I never personally was the target of his anger. Except for one time. We were in his office, and on his desk was one of those old-fashioned spindles, a spike Ida could use to impale messages or reminders. I noticed a few papers at the bottom of the spiked pile looked frayed and yellowed with age.

"Hey, Boss, don't you think it's about time you return some of those calls?" I asked, keeping my tone light. "You know, that guy must've called only two or three years ago."

He bristled. "Why the hell are you looking at papers on my desk? Tend to your own business!"

I was taken aback, but the moment passed. I learned that the man had boundaries. He didn't like to be pressured or second-guessed. It seemed only Ida could get away with giving him directives.

I remember when the daughter of a prominent Republican figure worked as a summer intern for a short period. She then applied for a job as an assistant district attorney in the DA's office. The applicant's mother was very recognizable in the metropolitan region for appearing in her company's ads. A longtime political insider, the mother was an associate of GOP Governor George Pataki and heavily involved in Republican politics. None of which would exactly endear her to a Kennedy Democrat like

Morgenthau. But the daughter should not be punished for the sins of the mother, and she should be given a fair shot at an ADA job.

Then came the barrage of calls in support of the daughter's appointment. Politicians and Albany bureaucrats weighed in, every contact the applicant's mover-and-shaker mother could ask. The situation became comical. Even I got a call imploring the young woman's hiring, and so did several others in the hierarchy of the office, all of us totally out of the loop as far as hiring decisions went. It was clearly overkill. If I were the daughter, I would have been embarrassed.

Morgenthau finally became fed up. As we walked back to the office after lunch, he stopped in his tracks when I told him of the mother's wheedling call.

"Fuck her!" Morgenthau bellowed. "Screw the girl and her damned mother. I'm not hiring her!" The favored scion of the political insider mother would have to find employment opportunities elsewhere.

Woe to the supplicant who would pressure, pester, or otherwise bother the Boss. He didn't appreciate people tugging on his sleeve. The man had his own ideas, one of which would shortly have a profound effect on my career.

Morgenthau realized early on that the office needed to run more efficiently so he decided to streamline the way cases would be handled. To accomplish this, he orchestrated a top to bottom reorganization of the DA's office.

The status quo, which was in place when I first started, might be labeled a vertical system. A case would come to us via an arrest by a beat cop or a detective, and a file was created and written up by an ADA in the complaint room. It would go to arraignment, where an ADA who staffed the arraignment part would handle it. More serious cases would be processed by the Indictment Bureau, where yet another ADA would deal with it and present the case to the grand jury.

Each case, in other words, would see a whole parade of assistant district attorneys, one for each stage of its journey through the court system. Every time a case reached a bureau, the ADA there would have to come up to speed on the particulars, which involved reviewing the original complaint and the write-ups, evidence, testimony, grand jury minutes, and other relevant documents.

The arrangement made little sense, except that it was a prime example of what is true of bureaucracies: *This is the way it's always been done.*

Morgenthau had a different idea. In the spring of 1976, he instituted a horizontal system of how cases should be handled. Under this new approach, the same ADA would follow a case, step by step, from the complaint room, now referred to as ECAB (Early Case Assessment Bureau) to indictment and eventually the presentation in court. No starting all over again from square one once a case left one stage of the process and entered another.

The reorganization rolled the Criminal Court Bureau, the Indictment Bureau, the Supreme Court Bureau, and the Homicide Bureau into a single trial bureau. With his top-to-bottom shakeup, Morgenthau in effect turned the prosecutorial system in Manhattan on its head. He created six trial bureaus, numbered 30, 40, 50, 60, 70 and 80. Each bureau was headed by a bureau chief and a deputy bureau chief, and staffed with ADAs with various levels of experience.

One spin-off from the reorganization was that murder cases would be handled in a slightly different manner. ADAs from the trial bureaus with relevant case experience would be assigned to "homicide call."

Murders were always treated as a major disturbance of "the Force," as they might say in *Star Wars*. There was nothing leisurely about their treatment within the system. When a murder came in, people snapped to attention. Homicide cases weren't set aside and scheduled within the framework of a five-day work week or an eight-hour day. Instead, the DA's office rotated assistant district attorneys assigned to handle homicide cases as they came in, around the clock. If you were the ADA on call, it was your case— although major cases that attracted media attention were usually assigned to senior ADAs. Being on homicide call meant you'd be on duty for a twenty-four-hour shift, basically remaining in a low-level state of anxiety all day and night. Sometimes you even had to go to the scene of the homicide.

My first time on homicide call came on the day of the Bicentennial, July 4, 1976. The office was closed. No one else was available. I had been an ADA in the office for less than two years. "What the hell? Am I going to be able to handle this thing alone if I get called?" I muttered to myself.

Luckily, my number never came up that day. I was glad that it didn't. But within a few months I would serve as the prosecutor on one of the most important murder cases of the era.

CHAPTER 7

FAMILY COURT

n 1977, New York was still embroiled in a fiscal crisis. It was also the year of the Son of Sam murders and a summer blackout that led to widespread looting in the city. I was assigned to Trial Bureau 60. Robert Seewald was my bureau chief. He was smart, experienced, had the patience of a saint, and never lost his cool. When I was a greenhorn ADA, Bob served as my advisor, my rabbi, my guru. I learned a lot from him. His temperament was such that we could sit down together, go over cases, and talk trial strategy. To this day, I consider him a friend and a mentor. Whenever he saw me anxious about a task, he'd take me aside and offer some advice and kind words.

"If you made a mistake, you'll make it up," he said. "You'll learn something. You'll make it right the next time."

Throughout this period, I prosecuted a lot of cases as an ADA. I accumulated courtroom experience, trying mostly robberies and burglaries. Property crime is the bread and butter of the criminal justice system. Assaults and attempted murders don't come up as often. I even tried a gambling case, which normally would have been assigned to the Rackets Bureau. In one of my first felony prosecutions, I tried and got a conviction on a rape case.

I was a foot soldier. It rarely means anything positive when a foot soldier gets a summons from the general. I was naturally a little perplexed when I heard Ida Van Lindt's voice on the phone one morning in October 1977.

"Mr. Morgenthau would like to see you," she said. "Can you meet with him this afternoon?" I didn't ask the reason for the call, and she didn't give me one. She merely noted the time when I was to present myself at the Boss's office on the eighth floor. Little did I know that this meeting would be a turning point in my career.

As usual, Morgenthau cut straight to the chase. "Would you be interested in handling felony cases involving juveniles in Family Court?"

That I was surprised doesn't quite say it. Dumbfounded, maybe, or flabbergasted. I would have liked to see a snapshot of my face taken at that moment. Where was this bolt out of the blue coming from?

Because I was caught up in my work as a freshly minted prosecutor in Trial Bureau 60, I hadn't kept up on the news as much as I probably should have. I concentrated on winning cases and getting bad people off the streets. There was a lot to learn. I kept my head down and my eyes on the prize, with the goal of becoming the best assistant district attorney and trial lawyer I could be. What did I know about new legal reforms passed by the legislature in Albany? All that was above my pay grade.

The age for adulthood in New York had always been sixteen years old. Before that age, juvenile offenders were processed through the Family Court system, which also handled divorce cases, custody cases, domestic disturbances, and similar matters. The arrangement was outdated and not really designed to tackle violent street crime and the increasingly complex problems of violent juvenile offenders in modern-day New York City. Family Court had long been behind the times, a nineteenth-century creation grappling with twentieth-century problems.

The ship of state tends to turn very slowly, but in those days, it was coming around. There was a movement afoot to address the uncomfortable reality of violent juvenile crime. Passed by the

New York legislature in 1976, the Juvenile Justice Reform Act (JJRA) provided mechanisms by which young offenders found guilty of serious crimes could be sentenced to "restrictive placement." That's legalese for *incarceration.*

Most relevant to my own situation, the law also allowed prosecutors from the district attorney's office into Family Court for the first time.

The Reform Act was a major reevaluation of the juvenile code, passed in response to public concern over an alarming increase in the frequency and seriousness of crime committed by youths. Before this, case law regarding children relied on the late nineteenth-century theory of juvenile reform. The most important element of the new law expanded the whole premise of the legal system's approach to treating underage offenders.

The guiding standard in Family Court criminal law had formerly been "the best interests of the youth." The Reform Act added another standard: "the concern for community protection."

There was a lot of chatter in those days about juvenile crime, and how young offenders were slipping through the system and being treated too lightly. The Reform Act extended the time that judges could sentence juvenile offenders, not to jail but to juvenile facilities. The new law created a "designated felony," which would be applied to serious crimes such as murder, rape, and robbery with a weapon.

Predictably, the new measure prompted a chorus of concern and handwringing. It was as if by employing restrictive placement for kids as young as thirteen in cases of murder, and as young as fourteen and fifteen for other serious crimes, we were putting them beyond the reach of rehabilitation. The idea violated the humanist faith in childhood innocence and the redemptive power of love, education, and mercy.

Still, cases involving violent juveniles kept coming. With

increasing frequency, the spectacle of young adolescents committing egregious offenses hit the tabloid newspapers and the evening news.

It took a while, but repercussions of the new, more violent urban realities spurred action in both Albany and the office of Governor Hugh Carey, a Democrat loath to be perceived as soft on crime. The political development simply addressed a changing landscape out on the streets. The phenomenon of kid killers, child rapists, and underage criminals was on the rise not just in New York City but nationwide. We had been asking a poorly equipped Family Court to deal with this new reality of violent juvenile offenders. Something had to be done.

Thus, the Juvenile Justice Reform Act of 1976 introduced a mandate that, for the first time, specified "designated felonies"— armed robbery, rape, sodomy, homicide, and attempted murder— be assigned to district attorney prosecutors in the Family Court. Like a chain reaction, what the lawmakers did in Albany filtered down to local district attorney offices, resulting in me sitting before Robert Morgenthau, fielding an offer for a new position.

"Gee, Boss, "I don't really know the first thing about Family Court," I blurted out.

He brushed aside my profession of ignorance. "I need someone who can create an entire new bureau from the ground up, staff it, formulate policies and procedures, get recordkeeping going . . . everything."

Morgenthau then launched into a five-minute thumbnail description of the recently passed Juvenile Justice Reform Act. I listened and tried to keep up.

"So what do you think?" he asked. "I'm looking for someone to head the unit, and I think you'd be a good choice."

I didn't know what to think. I asked myself, *Why me?* I had barely three years under my belt as an ADA. There were other assistants in the office who'd been there for much longer. I was assailed by negative thoughts buzzing in my mind. I wondered whether Morgenthau signaling me out meant this new position had to be one of limited significance, given my relative inexperience.

"I'm going to give you a secretary," Morgenthau said, as if the whole proposition was a done deal. "You'll have a couple of offices. And I'm going to give you two junior assistants to work with."

Too fast, I thought. The whole transfer was happening too fast. To this day, I don't know why I was appointed to head up the unit over more qualified and experienced ADAs Morgenthau could have chosen. I think Bob Seewald must have recommended me to Morgenthau, but he never informed me that he did.

I spoke to Seewald after getting the call from the Boss. I told him about my initial hesitation.

"I don't know the first thing about trying juveniles," I said.

"You'll be fine," Seewald responded, supportive as usual. "Don't worry. I have a lot of confidence you'll be able to handle whatever comes your way over there."

I still had doubts. "Over there" was 60 Lafayette Street, the building where Family Court was housed. I vaguely knew of the place, recognized it for its somewhat forbidding Brutalist architecture. The façade was just slabs of gray stone. The interior was a confusing labyrinth. The whole edifice did not exactly have a welcoming Sesame Street atmosphere for the children who were going to be processed there.

Another factor presented itself to me, a personal one rather than the professional doubts that had already arisen. In a strange coincidence, I would be transferring to a post in Family Court at the time when Shelley and I were planning to start a family. The thought of plunging myself into a legal milieu where kids were to be tried as adults unnerved me. At first, I had personal doubts about prosecuting juveniles as adults, even though they weren't facing the same penalties as adults or being incarcerated in the same facilities as adults. It just seemed strange for prosecutors to work in the family courts where there were no juries or other indicia of the criminal justice system.

I put my hesitation and doubts aside. I immediately studied the operation of Family Court, pondering how to start a unit for felony juvenile offenders within the existing structure. I had several meetings with Morgenthau to apprise him of my progress. At times we'd be joined by Peter Zimroth, his chief assistant, but mostly it was just me and the Boss. My relationship with the Boss developed—or, more accurately, we began to establish a personal relationship where none had existed before.

"What are we going to call this unit?" Morgenthau asked during one of our meetings. "We have to give it a name."

I had no clue. The state legislators hadn't labeled the new division. The venerable legislature of Albany had merely passed the Reform Act, leaving the nitty-gritty details to be worked out by someone else.

"How about the Juvenile Offense Bureau?" I suggested, totally off the cuff.

"J-O-B.," Morgenthau pronounced, trying the name on for size. He was a bureaucrat at heart, so he had a love of handy acronyms. "Juvenile Offense Bureau. That works."

"JOB," he said again. "I like it. Let's go with that."

I crossed the street, going from 100 Centre to 60 Lafayette, from Criminal Court to Family Court. I can't say that I was happy about it.

Aside from my mixed feelings, I instantly realized that the Family Court staffers matched my ambivalence and then some.

They didn't want prosecutors from the DA's office treading on their turf. I was considered an interloper from the hard-knock criminal court world, where justice was harsh and prison sentences were long. Family Court dealt mostly with "softer," non-criminal issues, such as divorce, adoption, and foster care. Trying young offenders was only a small part of its roster of services.

Family Court had its own way of doing things. Intentionally or not, the place was sealed off from the rest of the world, with a deep suspicion of outsiders. I was seen as a transplant from the big, bad world of prosecuting adults.

The powers that be assigned me two assistants: Catherine Cobb and Pat Hoey. They weren't happy with their new assignments either. They were both young ADAs who, like me, had been getting their feet wet in the criminal courts. To belabor the metaphor, Cobb and Hoey had been getting along swimmingly and now they found themselves in what they considered to be a backwater.

The idea of importing prosecutors into Family Court represented a controversial development. As trained ADAs operating within the purlieu of Family Court, we were breaking new ground.

We were not greeted with open arms. The judges, clerks, and administrators didn't want us there. We had no friends. The attitude was, "You hotshots are going to swagger in here and think you're going to put things right? Well, we don't need you. We're doing just fine on our own, thank you very much."

Morgenthau had tasked me with a massive administrative task: building a new trial bureau from the ground up. I had to formulate a whole new set of procedures and develop policies to deal with the new, recently created class of criminal offenses, "designated felonies." I had to keep track of the cases as they progressed through the system. There were no juries. All the cases were essentially bench trials, decided by judges alone.

I also had to learn a whole new legal vocabulary to work with in Family Court. Arraignment, for example, was called "intake." Defendants were labeled "respondents." What we were doing was not termed a trial but a "fact-finding hearing." A guilty verdict was not a conviction but a "finding."

The term "prosecutor" was never used in Family Court. Because they represented the concerns of the city, cases had always been handled by the staff of the Corporation Counsel's office—the corporation in this case being the city of New York. The New York City Corporation Counsel was one person, appointed by the mayor, who directed hundreds of lawyers and other personnel.

Except in the Family Court division, the Corporation Counsel does not usually operate in the realm of criminal prosecution. The office deals in civil litigation, including lawsuits against the city and the lawsuits mounted by the city. The Corporation Counsel really didn't have the experience or the tools to handle serious cases. They weren't familiar with criminal prosecution, with hearings, lineups, and procedures commonplace across the street at 100 Centre.

That's why the New York State legislature mandated creation of what became the Juvenile Offense Bureau, which would focus on the kind of violent crimes that were outside the normal realm of the Family Court.

I made a crucial decision early on. I would not come on like gangbusters, and I directed Cobb and Hoey likewise to tread carefully. What are the sensible first moves for the new sheriff in town? Listen. Observe. Learn.

The strategy worked. Slowly but surely, I was able to befriend the clerks and deal with the judges. The personnel realized that Hoey, Cobb, and I were not monsters. We were basically decent people. I think the Family Court staffers realized deep down that the system they operated in could not effectively deal with some of the cases that were coming their way.

After two years prosecuting violent adults, I thought I had seen it all. I thought I knew the truth of the Latin expression, *homini homo lupus,* "man is wolf to man." It turned out there was something new under the sun. I modified the Latin to *pueri et lupus est:* "A child can be a wolf also."

I remember the case that drove the point home. The details were horrific. A gang of kids dragged a boy up to the roof of a tenement building. They beat him, shoved pebbles up his rectum, and lit his hair on fire.

Ruthless and extreme, yes, but I had already encountered extremes in adult court. What was new to me was the child perpetrator's absolute lack of remorse. There seemed to be something missing in the moral makeup of their character. Contrition wasn't in the cards. They displayed no emotion, no feeling that they had committed a terrible act. Across the street at 100 Centre, the adults I prosecuted at least *pretended* to be remorseful.

The experience changed me. Depressed me. I felt desperate to shield my loved ones from the harsh, unforgiving world I was facing. Adults committing crimes was one thing. Youths perpetrating the same crimes added a whole new level of moral complexity.

As the year 1977 bled into 1978—and sometimes the metaphor was literal—Cobb, Hoey, and I ramped up JOB and handled cases. The workload was fairly light compared to the criminal courts across the street. We rejected some designated felonies and sent them back to the existing system. Other cases settled without formal proceedings, with the judge, attorneys, and all concerned agreeing to the terms of the penalty. In a few instances, we went to trial, or rather, we held a hearing.

I still wasn't happy with my new assignment, but I was pleased that I had the new bureau up and running. I could not have foreseen a new case coming down the pike that would explode into the public consciousness, one that would change my career, as well as alter the course of criminal justice going forward.

CHAPTER 8

KNEE-TO-KNEE WITH EVIL

T he spring of 1978 represented the bad old days in New York City. Crime was rampant. The quality of life in the city deteriorated. The city still flirted with bankruptcy and didn't have the funds to conduct normal government operations. The situation hit public transportation especially hard.

The money simply wasn't there to keep the subways clean and safe. Every other train car seemed to be tagged with graffiti over every square inch. The claustrophobic, nowhere-to-run nature of the subway made the transit system a crime victim's nightmare. Commuters had to watch their backs. Petula Clark's 1967 hit song, "Don't Sleep in the Subway" took on ominous new overtones.

In the late afternoon on March 19, 1978, a fifteen-year-old named William Bosket, Jr., known as Willie, and his eighteen-year-old cousin, Herman Spates, cruised the New York City subway system looking for targets to rob. The two had committed such robberies often. Their method was simple: search the trains for sleeping passengers alone in a car, then "accidentally" kick their intended targets in passing, and if the marks didn't wake up, rifle their pockets for money.

Around 5:30 p.m. on the number 3 IRT train, Bosket and Spates found Noel Perez, a forty-forty-year-old Bronx hospital worker who had been unlucky or incautious enough to have fallen asleep. Bosket noticed Perez wearing what appeared to be an expensive digital watch.

As he slipped the prize off Perez's wrist, the mark opened his eyes.

It should have ended there. Spates and Bosket could have taken off, punched the guy to foil pursuit, or left him behind to search for other slumbering victims. But Willie Bosket was a special case. He idolized his absent father, William Bosket, Sr., a.k.a. "Butch," who was in prison at the time for committing a double murder in a Milwaukee pawnshop.

Willie Bosket's early years weren't much of a childhood at all, just a steady string of tragic incidents, state-sponsored attempts at rehabilitation, and numerous frightening, impulsive, volcanic explosions of anger that resulted in violent assaults and serious injuries to others. He was a child not of a stable family but of the streets.

Just a few weeks before he stood over Noel Perez on the 3 train, Willie Bosket spent sixty-five dollars of robbery money for a .22 pistol that he'd bought from his mother's boyfriend. When Noel Perez woke up to see the kid yanking off his watch, Bosket leveled the gun and shot him through his right eye. Fearing that it would not fully finish off a potential witness, Willie shot another bullet into Perez's left temple.

Eight days later, on March 27, Spates and Bosket were again back on the hunt on the 3 train, and Bosket murdered again. The second victim, Moises Perez, had the same last name as the first, but they were not related. Two one-dollar bills represented the total score for the second murder.

Willie Bosket was eight months shy of his sixteenth birthday.

After he was arrested for the subway killings and a later attempted murder of a subway motorman, I stood in Family Court tasked with protecting the public from Willie Bosket. Because he was under sixteen years old—the age of adulthood under New

York state law—the judicial system dealt with Bosket's crimes differently than if he had been an adult. Even after the Juvenile Justice Reform Act was passed in 1976, it became clear that violent juvenile offenders were a growing problem for which the justice system was ill-prepared.

Willie Bosket was a poster boy for the idea that more measures were necessary to address the current situation. A fifteen-year-old subway murderer? Whoever heard of such a thing?

When I saw Willie Bosket in court, it gave rise to a feeling I had never experienced before, despite my years of prosecuting criminals of all stripes. I became convinced that I had come face to face with an individual so violent, so dangerous, so out of control that he could not be allowed to roam the streets.

The concept of an evil human being can be a difficult pill to swallow. We all want to believe that no one is out of the reach of goodness, that no one is beyond rehabilitation or cannot be saved. To all those who hold tight to such high-minded beliefs, I ask the simple and direct question: What are you going to do with someone like Willie Bosket?

At that time, second-in-command in the Corporation Counsel hierarchy was a feisty thirty-six-year-old Brooklyn-born woman named Judith Sheindlin. A friendly, energetic, no-nonsense force of nature, Judy was very knowledgeable about the law and the juvenile justice system. She liked to pepper anyone with experience in the court system with questions. She was a go-getter, constantly seeking information that would help in her quest to be a better lawyer.

All that never-say-die drive would serve Judy well. In a few years Mayor Ed Koch would elevate her to the position of a Family Court judge, and a few years after that, with her own courtroom reality TV show, she would become world-famous as Judge Judy.

A 2013 *Reader's Digest* poll found that Americans trusted Judge Judy more than all nine justices of the United States Supreme Court.

But in 1977, she was still just plain old Judy Sheindlin when she buttonholed me one day in the Family Court building. She asked if I had heard about Willie Bosket, a kid who was a legend in the Family Court system.

It turned out I already had. Marty Davin, an NYPD detective whom I had worked with on felony cases in the criminal courts, had caught the Perez-Perez subway murders. He was working with a transit cop named Nick Vasquez. Employing good old-fashioned shoe-leather police work, the duo had collared both Bosket and his older cousin, Herman Spates. Davin filled me in on the sad and sobering saga of Willie Bosket's decade-and-a-half on earth.

The family was broken. His father, Butch, was in prison for a double homicide, and his entire family had a long history of violence. His mother Laura just barely kept her head above water, a single mom locked in poverty. Willie was a sociopath: sweet, smiling, and endearing one minute and an exploding volcano in the next. Bosket was described by counselors as "a beautiful child," "smart, with an IQ of 130," "a great opportunity for rehabilitation," but also as a crazed kid with a hair-trigger temper who would "grow up to kill." He was in and out of juvenile detention facilities since his grade school years, one after another: Wiltwyck, Brookwood, Spofford, the Kennedy home, the Manhattan Youth Development Center.

His behavior went well beyond juvenile mischief. Since childhood, Bosket liked to set fire to people's beds—with the occupants in them. One of his therapists quit the social welfare system when Bosket stood over her while she was pregnant, holding a chair above his head, about to crash it down on her. Violence was often Bosket's preferred mode of communication.

"This one should definitely not be on the outside," Judy Sheindlin warned me. "He's coming up in front of Phil Thurston for an intake hearing. I'm terrified that a judge like Thurston is going to put him right back out on the streets. He'll let the kid out, especially since he has roots in the community."

Family Court was notorious for its revolving-door justice. Cases were often dismissed by probation officers at intake. Juvenile offenders would come before a judge again and again, have their cases dropped, the charges lowered or dismissed, or be put into the care of a relative. Judge Phillip Thurston was one of those jurists who bent over backward to give juvenile offenders every break in the world.

"Listen, Bob," Judy said to me. "Everything I hear about Bosket is that he's very good at fooling people, especially judges. He's good looking when he smiles, very handsome and well-spoken, very ingratiating. He can be really personable. He can take you in. And then, it's like a switch is flipped. Then you can see he is like Jekyll and Hyde—the anger, the frustration, the violence."

I told Judy that I had heard much the same story from Detective Marty Davin. Davin described Bosket as tough and smart, with absolutely no respect for authority. When arrested, he lashed out at Davin, using the language of the streets.

"You've got shit on me!" Bosket had shouted.

Judy grabbed me by the sleeve to emphasize the weight of her words. "I'm serious, Bob. This child cannot go back onto the streets. Do not let that happen. He's going to kill more people."

I took the future Judge Judy's advice to heart when I entered Bosket's intake hearing before Judge Thurston. Present were the judge, a stenographer, a court clerk, two court officers, and Bosket's

Legal Aid attorney, Kay McNally, plus his hard-bitten probation officer, Seymour Gottfried. Gottfried had also reinforced what both Detective Davin and Judge Judy had said, that Willie Bosket was a tough case.

That day in court I saw the charisma that everyone was talking about. I didn't see the rage, not at first, but there was something hidden or cloaked in the way Bosket carried himself.

Kay McNally impressed me. In fact, almost every Legal Aid lawyer I came up against in Family Court seemed dedicated and committed. As overworked and underpaid as they were, I always found them to be very devoted to their clients. In her forties, a consummate professional, Kay was a good advocate for Bosket.

"Mr. Bosket lives at home with his mother and sister," was McNally's argument to Thurston. "He was there when the police officers came, and he didn't run away. We'll know where to find him, Your Honor."

Thurston, a bald man in his sixties with a tonsure of white hair ringing the sides of his head, was a long-standing Family Court judge known for this type of logic and lending a sympathetic ear. As I approached him, I couldn't tell where he stood on the question of letting Willie out.

"We are dealing with a very dangerous person," I said. "Your Honor, he must be remanded to a secure facility. If you let him loose, he will commit more acts of violence."

I did my darndest to make sure Judge Thurston knew the gravity of the situation. All the while I monitored Bosket out of the corner of my eye, just in case he took offense at my remarks.

You have to understand that a Family Court facility is nothing like the expansive courtrooms seen on TV and in movies. Those are the palaces of the criminal justice system. Family Court proceedings occur in small spaces, with a feel more like a living room than a courtroom. There is no gallery, no multiple rows of seats for spectators. The judge sits elevated behind a counter-like bench. The participants are arranged side by side in a vague sort of horseshoe—four chairs here, another four chairs there, no more than three or four feet apart and separated by a narrow middle aisle.

Bosket sat just few feet away from me, next to McNally. I could have reached out and touched him, and he could have reached out and done more than touch me. I was not only face-to-face with evil; I was now knee-to-knee with it too.

Thurston was one of those judges who seemed offended by the presence of a professional prosecutor in his courtroom. Although he came off as annoyed with me, he yielded to the weight of my argument rather than Kay McNally's. With some reluctance, the judge kept Bosket in what passed for jail in the juvenile justice system: the Manhattan Youth Development Center. I think Thurston recognized that if Bosket had gotten out and committed another crime, he might find himself looking bad in the pages of the tabloids.

Those tabloids promoted the Willie Bosket story with a vengeance, running front-page stories labeling him the "Baby-Faced Killer." I knew journalists would be hot on this case. Even if I hadn't come to that conclusion by myself, I would have been told by the higher-ups.

Peter Zimroth, second-in-command to Morgenthau, reached out to me by phone. "Bob, please be sure to give me a call every morning or so, just to keep me apprised of the Bosket case."

During the Thurston intake hearing, I saw the "baby-faced" side of Willie Bosket on full display. He was calm and collected in court. But as the proceedings against him continued in Family Court, I caught glimpses of the other side of him: the violent killer side.

In criminal courtrooms, there are usually four court officers present to keep order. Not in Family Court, where the city kept a smaller staff. The two officers present on the first day of the Bosket proceeding looked big enough, but there were only two. *These guys better be on their toes,* I remember thinking to myself. I feared Bosket might make a run for it.

Besides, who knew what the boy had in his pocket? Security at Family Court was famously lax. Before he used the .22 pistol to murder the two Perez victims, Bosket's weapon of choice was a knife. Specifically, he carried a switchblade, also called a gravity knife or, in street slang, a 007 after James Bond's handle.

I never took my eyes off him the entire time we were in court.

After Judge Thurston remanded Bosket, one of the initial proceedings in Bosket's case was a so-called "Huntley hearing" on the admissibility of statements made during the first police interview.

The hearing took place in front of Supervisory Judge Edith Miller, sitting in Part Four, the section of Family Court dedicated to designated felonies. An impeccably dressed, devoutly religious woman, Judge Miller genuinely devoted herself to helping young people who came before her. She took a great interest in setting them on the right path.

But she had never run into anyone like Willie Bosket. I could tell that Miller, an African American woman approaching her sixtieth year, was uncomfortable with Bosket as a defendant. She was accustomed to milder cases than his. In this initial preliminary hearing, Judge Miller had to rule whether statements Bosket gave when he was arrested by Davin would be admitted in subsequent proceedings.

The question I always posed when I fielded a homicide call was an instance of cop-speak. "Is the defendant warmed up?" I would ask, wanting to know if the perp had given statements and was ready for a Q-and-A with an ADA.

Harvey Rosen had taken the call when Bosket was arrested. A tall, thin ADA with a wispy beard, he always conjured up an image of Don Quixote in my mind, the Man of La Mancha. At this hearing before Miller, Rosen detailed how the supposedly very smart Willie Bosket tripped himself up. During his post-arrest jailhouse interview, Bosket had sworn to Rosen that he'd never shot either Moises or Noel Perez. But then he slipped up and admitted he had found the .22 murder weapon on the street and had it in his possession during the time when the murders were committed.

In this first interview encounter with Bosket, Rosen was chilled by a threat the boy threw at him. "I wouldn't use a gun on you," Bosket had said to Rosen. "If I was going to do anything to you, I'd use a knife."

Detective Marty Davin, who had also been present during the first jailhouse interview, testified at the hearing. Davin told the court about finding the murder weapon hidden in the Bosket family apartment on West 145th Street in Harlem. Davin was silver-haired, a little chunky at five-foot-nine, one of those old-style Irish cops who were always smiling or laughing. He used his smile to try to get under Bosket's skin, not really needling Willie outright, but trying to manipulate him to show his violent side.

It worked. Bosket blew a gasket. "He's a fucking liar!" he screamed, leaping up and pointing at Davin. "He's full of shit!"

This was what Detective Davin wanted all along. There are no juries in Family Court. The judge solely decided the case. So Davin wanted to show Judge Miller who Willie Bosket was in all the young killer's unhinged glory.

After Bosket's outburst, the courtroom erupted, and the two court officers rushed to subdue him. Judge Miller was taken aback by his sudden rage. Kay McNally, his lawyer, was like a lion tamer.

One of her great skills was always being able to calm her client down.

The hearing was adjourned for three days. I realized we had a looming problem. Laura Bosket, Willie's mother, had led the police to the murder weapon. She was obviously frightened of her raging bull of a son.

"We don't want the mother to testify that she turned the gun over," Rosen had told me. He was afraid of the repercussions should Bosket discover his mom had betrayed him.

When the proceeding resumed three days later, Kay McNally called Laura to the stand for the defense. The woman denied that she guided police to where the gun was hidden. "The cops came in," she testified. "They searched the house, and they found the gun."

Bosket was not happy when I cross-examined Laura. He became very agitated when his mother was on the stand. As I finished, Bosket leaped to his feet.

"I'm gonna kill you both—you Judge and you Mr. DA!" he shouted, pointing his finger at me and Judge Miller.

Nothing like this had ever happened before to Judge Miller. I knew she was afraid of Bosket. In her heart of hearts, she felt that he was capable of doing exactly what he promised. I could feel my blood pressure rising. I realized I was dealing with a fifteen-year-old sociopath.

The court officers again led the unruly Bosket out of court. As they took him, he turned around, glaring at me, and shouted, "Fuck you!" Then spat at me.

I felt prepared on the day I was to present the prosecution's case at the fact-finding hearing. I had my witnesses assembled, including Davin, Rosen, a ballistics expert, and the spouses of the deceased victims. Herman Spates had agreed to testify against Bosket as part of a plea deal.

Then Kay McNally walked in and dropped a bombshell.

"Willie wants to plead guilty," she whispered to me in a low voice. I could not believe my ears. I knew this kid as a fighter all the way. Suddenly, Bosket was stripping off his boxing gloves and throwing them to the floor, declaring "I quit."

Bosket wanted to "end all this bullshit." I eventually concluded that he wanted to shield his cousin from having to testify against him. Bosket didn't want Spates going to prison with a "snitch" label attached to him.

Judge Miller sentenced the young murderer to the maximum under the law, which for juvenile offenders was five years in a "secure" facility. Bosket was released a little over four years later. He went right back to his criminal ways, committed violent felonies as an adult, and wound up in prison for life.

Before that happened, Bosket came looking for me. In 1982, during his brief hiatus of freedom, he showed up in a restricted area of the Family Court building. Eric Pomerantz, one of the ADAs, spotted the twenty-year-old Bosket without recognizing who he was.

"Can I help you?" Pomerantz had asked.

"I'm looking for Bob Silbering."

"Who are you?"

"My name's Willie Bosket."

The name didn't ring any bells with Pomerantz, and he told Bosket that I didn't work there anymore. Later on, Pomerantz mentioned the odd incident to another ADA, Robert Anesi, who knew exactly who Willie Bosket was.

All hell broke loose. I walked into the office the next morning to find two detectives waiting for me. For the next three weeks, they were my constant companions, accompanying me everywhere. I was also given a bulletproof vest, which my wife, Shelley, made sure I put on every morning before I left the house. I wonder how many other husbands left their families on their way to work wearing a bulletproof vest. A few weeks later, Bosket was arrested for, and later convicted of, the robbery of an elderly man. This was the first in a series of crimes that led to him being sentenced to life in prison.

A brutal coda appended itself to the Bosket story. In 1988, I received a phone call from a young reporter for a local newspaper in Utica, a town in upstate New York. Matt Worth had first encountered Bosket while covering one of his many appearances in court.

"I'm doing a story about Willie," Worth told me on the phone. "I'm going up to see him in prison." At that point in time, the state held Bosket in Shawangunk Correctional Facility in Wallkill, New York.

"I know you had Willie in Family Court," Worth said. "Is there anything you can tell me about him?"

I wondered if Worth knew what he was getting himself into. "The only thing I'm going to tell you is to be very careful," I said. "Don't be taken in by him. He's a handsome guy, well-spoken. But he's a con man."

I recognized how hard it was to warn reporters off when they're on the scent of a story. "Are you sure you really want to have this meeting with him?"

"I'm going to go up," Worth said. "I've already spoke with him and the prison officials."

"You have to do what you have to do, but I'm telling you, don't trust him." I recalled Bosket's fury in court, lashing out, threatening to kill me and Judge Miller. "He's like a volcano. He can erupt at any time."

All my fears came true. Worth went to Shawangunk, and while he was sitting in the visiting room, Bosket pulled out a homemade weapon and stabbed Earl Porter, a correctional officer, in the chest. The metal shank, improvised from a part of a bedframe, missed Porter's heart by inches. He survived, and Bosket had another sentence added to his jail term.

Prison officials placed Bosket in a custom-made cell, its steel bars contained within a shell of Plexiglass, Hannibal Lecter-style, so that correction officers could monitor him twenty-four hours a day. To my knowledge, he was the only prisoner in the New York State prison system who was incarcerated in this type of specialized environment. But he must have aged out of his young man's fury; at the time of this writing, officials have transferred him to a medium security prison.

In the wake of publicity of the Bosket case, in 1978 the New York State legislature passed the Juvenile Offender Act, which allowed the justice system to try violent juvenile offenders as adults. The measure was so intimately associated with the fifteen-year-old killer that it was forever known as "the Willie Bosket Law."

Not only did Bosket's murders serve as the impetus for the new legislation, but so did another front-page case that I tried in Family Court. The so-called "Laughing Boy Murder" happened in July 1978, only months after the Perez-Perez subway killings.

Thirteen-year-old Felipe Olave and another older friend encountered two young teens on 135th Street in Morningside Heights. Olave had just moved into the area. He was short, about five feet tall, and liable to be picked on, so he felt he had to prove himself in the new neighborhood. Olave carried a .22 caliber pistol, and a firearm always changes the equation in every situation.

Hugh McEvoy, a fifteen-year-old seminary student, was sitting on a railing outside Columbia University with a friend, Peter Maher. He happened to laugh as Olave passed by.

"What are you laughing at?" Olave asked.

"We're not laughing at anything," responded Maher.

The senseless question and his friend's reply represented the last words McEvoy ever heard. Olave aimed his gun at McEvoy, but the gun misfired. He stopped, twisted the cylinder, and pulled the trigger again. This time, McEvoy took a single bullet in the head. He passed away four days later.

The victim's parents, Leo and Elizabeth, demonstrated a remarkable degree of magnanimity in the face of their son's death. The McEvoys donated their son's eyes and kidneys to organ recipients. "In many ways, although our son died, he'll continue to live in that respect," said Leo McEvoy. Both parents of the victim pleaded for mercy for the killer.

"Our son loved everyone he came in contact with," Leo said. "His attitude would be one of forgiveness. Christ said, 'turn the other cheek,' and that's what one has to do to be a Christian." Elizabeth McEvoy said she hoped the criminal justice system could "do something" for Olave. "If he needs help, he should get it. I feel sorry for his mother."

Leo added that he believed the murderer should have every chance at redemption. Young killers should be "given the opportunity to rehabilitate themselves if that's what they really want to do." I don't think I or most other people would react in that way to a murder of someone near and dear to us.

When Olave was brought to Family Court to face charges, an aura of tragedy permeated the whole proceeding. If Bosket represented the worst offender I ever came up against, then the McEvoy-Olave case was the saddest I ever encountered. If I had dealt with the devil in Willie Bosket, I felt I was dealing with an angel with McEvoy. As bad a kid as Bosket was, that was how good McEvoy was.

The two cases, coming on the heels of one another, represented a one-two punch that forced a change in laws regarding violent juvenile offenders. Three days before the McEvoy killing, New York Governor Hugh Carey weighed in on the Bosket case. "I'm going to make sure that kid never gets out of prison," he told reporters. After McEvoy hit the headlines, Carey summoned the legislature back into session, demanding new laws be passed to sentence juvenile felons as adults.

Carey's Juvenile Offender Act of 1978 incorporated the most radical and controversial amendments to New York's juvenile crime statutes in decades. For the first time since 1909, thirteen-year-olds could be prosecuted as adults for murder. Fourteen- and fifteen-year olds could be prosecuted as adults for murder and other serious felonies. The gradual decriminalization of what used to be termed juvenile delinquency, a process which began over a century ago, had been reversed.

The pendulum of justice swings back and forth in response to changing realities. But in truth, everything old is new again. On December 11, 2019, just blocks away from where Felipe Olave killed Hugh McEvoy, fourteen-year-old Rashaun Weaver took the life of eighteen-year-old Tessa Majors. He stabbed the Barnard College student to death while his partner in crime, fourteen-year-old Luchiano Lewis, held her in a headlock. Both were tried as adults and convicted. It was Willie Bosket and Felipe Olave all over again.

In the progressive atmosphere of today, there's a pushback against the juvenile offender laws of 1976 and 1978. The public mood now swings the other way. There's a present trend toward once again considering what's best for the child, rather than the interests of public safety. But after all is said and done, the question still remains:

What are we going to do with a person like Willie Bosket? Felipe Olave? Rashaun Weaver?

Some sectors of the public want to remove law enforcement

from the social equation. They say that such an extreme move will effectively solve any problem. Defund the police, empty the prisons, place restrictions on the justice system. In place of a public safety response to crime, substitute rehabilitation for incarceration, and let's have social workers respond to 911 calls.

Recently, many district attorney candidates across the country ran on such policy platforms. Candidates spent their time trying to out-progressive each other. The aggressive number of social programs they proposed made me think that they were really running to put themselves out of a job. The progressive wanna-be DAs will take office and have nothing to do, since all of society's problems will be solved before they ever land in court. Do they really understand what they will encounter when they take office?

The trouble with this approach is that law enforcement, public safety, and the justice system are by nature reactive, not proactive. We are not social workers. Prosecutors get involved once the crime is committed. There are very few proactive steps that prosecutors can take. Prosecutors can support the Police Athletic League (as Robert Morgenthau did in NYC) or go into classrooms to talk to students. We can set up programs to deal with individual cases, such as we did in Special Narcotics, with DTAP (Drug Treatment Alternatives to Prison). But such measures will never represent a very large part of what we do.

Again, for the most part, prosecutors react to crimes that have already been committed. Our job is to seek justice, protect the innocent, and defend society against abuses by prosecuting the guilty. The progressive district attorney candidates want to challenge that basic reality. In fact, many of them propose to altogether halt the prosecution of misdemeanors, such as resisting arrest, fare jumping, prostitution, and other infractions.

These "reforms" represent the direct opposite approach to the "broken windows" theory of policing, whereby minor offenses are addressed vigorously. When put in place by Police Commissioner William Bratton in New York City in the mid 90's, the "broken windows" tactic proved effective in driving down crime rates.

In place of the natural *reactive* stance of crime control, the progressives propose *proactive* policies, programs that will supposedly prevent crimes before they happen. I'm sorry, but that is simply not the prosecutor's job. Such measures will exhaust scarce resources with no real guarantee they will be effective in reducing violent crime. Some activists seek to reduce the prison population by prosecuting serious felonies as misdemeanors. They labor under the misperception that they are making the streets safer by not sending felons to prison. It is difficult to believe that some progressive DAs will institute policies of not incarcerating repeat felony offenders who commit serious crimes.

To all those who advocate the magic answer of increased social programs to address the issue of violent crime, I always come back to the same question, feeling the urge to raise the same concern. It's a very real question, simple, direct, and—within the framework of progressive policy—unanswerable.

What are you going to do with someone like Willie Bosket?

Politically, I am a registered Independent, with no allegiance to either party. I vote based on the candidates and their positions on the issues. But when some well-meaning progressive argues that all human beings who do wrong can be rehabilitated, and that ugly, impoverished childhoods can explain all criminality, I have to respectfully disagree. I'm all for second chances. But Willie Bosket had second, third, and fourth chances in his life, and he wound up doing nothing with them.

CHAPTER 9

JUDGES AND JURIES

"**T**he law is an ass," states Charles Dickens. "First thing we do is kill all the lawyers," writes Shakespeare. We all know that lawyer jokes get passed around like candy. It's easy to mock the law, scorn it, attack it. In the face of all that, I'll always keep my faith in the rule of law as a force of order in a chaotic world.

As I've stated before, the legal system is not perfect, but nothing human is. The blindfold on the statue representing the idea that justice is blind might slip a bit, especially when there is big money involved. But the legal profession as I know it is overwhelmingly populated with good, honest people trying to do the best they can in the quest for justice.

In fall of 1978, I received a summons to see the Boss. I had been in Family Court for just under a year, organizing and heading up the Juvenile Offense Bureau.

I headed over to Morgenthau's office on the eighth floor of the Criminal Courts building. He started talking before I even had a chance to sit down.

"You know Gene is the bureau chief over there in thirty," Morgenthau said.

I had to fill in the gaps myself. "Gene" was Eugene Porcaro, Bureau Chief of Trial Bureau 30, one of six trial bureaus within the DA's office that prosecuted cases in both the Criminal Court and the New York County Supreme Court. He had been the deputy bureau chief but was recently promoted when the previous bureau chief left the DA's office.

I knew Porcaro to be quite an eccentric character, someone who enjoyed self-deprecating humor. He lived in an upscale neighborhood in Westchester, but he enjoyed telling stories about how much he loved a good bargain. He used to go to a store named Damages to buy clothing that somehow had flaws or was unfit for the sales racks. One day I found him wearing a monogrammed shirt, but I didn't recognize the stitched-on letters.

"Gene, those aren't your initials," I said.

"I know," he responded, "but I only paid two dollars for this shirt!"

Gene would wear ludicrously garish outfits at his annual holiday party, clashing plaid jackets and pants. If someone asked him about one of his outfits, we already knew his trademark reply: "I only paid five bucks for this!" Joking aside, Gene was an excellent bureau chief who was liked and respected by his assistants.

That day in his office, Morgenthau explained that Porcaro, as a trial bureau chief, did not have the time to run the bureau on a full-time basis because he was busy with a big case involving a supermarket shooting and robbery.

"Gene is in court four days a week, so he needs someone to help him out," Morgenthau said.

"Boss, are you offering me a deputy bureau chief spot?" I asked, not quite believing my ears.

I was overjoyed at the prospect. As much as I liked getting things into shape at Family Court, I yearned to be back at 100 Centre where the real action was. I had spent many happy days as an ADA there, and it would be a joy to return to it, with a promotion to boot.

I realized Morgenthau appreciated my work in organizing the Juvenile Offense Bureau and tackling tough cases like Bosket and

Olave. He would never come right out and tell me, but I knew my success there resulted in my getting the promotion.

"It would really be more than the usual deputy spot," Morgenthau told me. "Basically, you'd pretty much have to run the show."

I accepted the position, of course. The trial taking up Porcaro's time concerned a sensational supermarket robbery gone wrong, resulting in shots fired, a homicide, and murder charges. I had heard about the case and knew the judge, State Supreme Court Justice Clifford Scott. His nickname was "Maximum Scott" because he liked to deliver heavy sentences.

My new boss, Gene Porcaro, was in court on trial most of the time. His leadership still provided a virtually friction-less work environment. My duties as his second-in-command most resembled that of an air traffic controller, as I kept track of the dozens of cases that came into the bureau every week, making sure everything ran smoothly. I assigned ADAs to cover the criminal and supreme court parts, and was available to consult on cases and court presentations and discuss plea bargaining offers. My days were packed, but enjoyably so.

I never believed in too many meetings. If there was a problem, I would much rather handle it one-on-one. If we had to discuss an upcoming proceeding, or when word came down that the courts wanted cases handled a certain way, I'd assemble the ADAs and hash out the issue. Of course there were times when we needed to have a bureau meeting with all the assistants to discuss a new office or bureau policy or any other issues that needed to be addressed. Occasionally, I would go to court to see how it was going with a few of the assistants on trial. I didn't really like sitting at a desk.

I always favored a personal, hands-on approach. I made my rounds every day, visiting offices and stopping in to see people. I tried to make human connections, asking how their families were or schmoozing about local sports teams. There wasn't anything calculating about this approach—it simply marked my natural personality. I was a people person. I'd often leave folks on a positive note.

"You're the best," was a line I used a lot, and at times I got called on it.

"Hey, you tell everyone they're the best!" an assistant or staffer might joke.

"Well, you are the best of the best!" I'd respond.

As the Deputy Bureau Chief in Trial Bureau 30, I got along well with the bureau's thirty-five ADAs, the staff, and the other personnel with whom I interacted. Even the judges (most of them) didn't appear to be ogres.

At the deputy bureau chief level, you don't get to try cases in court all that often. I missed it. I wanted to make sure I didn't lose my trial skills. Managing a busy office of a couple of dozen assistant district attorneys is one thing, but there's nothing like presenting a case in court, which combines the sensations of tightrope walking, a debating contest, and a gladiatorial battle, with a little dramatic improvisation mixed in.

I found it exciting to be back in the criminal court arena. Given some of the tragic cases I had been dealing with in Family Court, the criminal activity I confronted did not seem more extreme just because it happened among adults.

Just as in any profession, there are varying levels of competence and expertise in the legal arena. I formed the opinion that some of the judges I encountered should never have been selected for the bench at all. Others were solid and professional, and a few were outstanding and well respected. There were those who were weak and allowed defense attorneys to take over the courtroom. Others were strong, with an excellent sense of command over trial procedures. Some didn't know criminal law, and some knew it inside and out. There were judges who didn't like to sentence defendants to long periods of incarceration, favoring the defense bar, and others who favored the prosecution and meted out heavy sentences.

I could never understand the logic behind the practice of electing judges rather than appointing them. I always thought judges running for office opened the door to all sorts of negative outcomes. Nowadays, some judicial election campaigns spend millions of dollars. If I could name a single thing that would most likely skew the course of justice, it would be placing partisan hacks on the bench. Judges should be selected on merit, recommended by legal committees or bar associations, bodies that are knowledgeable about the character and experience of the various candidates.

The infamous attorney Roy Cohn used a line that expressed a germ of truth about the justice system. "When a client comes to me, I never want to know what the charges are," Cohn said. "The first question I ask is who is the judge."

More than any prosecutor or defense lawyer, judges set the tone for what happens in a trial. Judges can be stern, learned, ignorant, clever, lackadaisical, proactive, reserved, fast, slow, funny, humorless, alert, or sleepy. They can establish the mood and pacing of a trial as surely as a conductor can direct an orchestra.

I tried a case before Judge Scott. The defendant, named Byrd, worked in a nursing home. His mother got into an argument one night with a neighbor. Later that night, someone broke into the neighbor's apartment and shot her five times. She lived and staggered two blocks to the local hospital.

"It was dark," the victim testified in court. "But I could see that it was Byrd who shot me."

The lawyer put up an alibi defense that Byrd could not have committed the crime because he had been at home with his wife and kids when the shooting occurred. Byrd knew this for a fact, since he recalled watching his favorite TV show, the police crime drama *S.W.A.T.*

Hmmm, I thought. I was aware of the show, well-known for its excessive displays of violence. In preparation for my cross-examination of Byrd, I had gotten my hands on a *TV Guide* for the evening in question. I discovered that *S.W.A.T.* had been preempted that night for a showing of the Sidney Poitier–Rod Steiger classic, *In the Heat of the Night.*

I had Byrd dead to rights. His alibi, flimsy as it was, didn't hold up. I didn't want to tip my hand, so I tried not to act like the cat who ate the canary as I questioned him. My cross-examination went something like this:

Me: Mr. Byrd, is that what you do every Saturday night, watch *S.W.A.T.*?

Byrd: Well, yes, that night we watched that.

Me: Can you tell me who the star of the show is?

Byrd: Steve Forrest.

I left it there and went on to another subject before circling back.

Me: Let's go back to you watching *S.W.A.T.* for a minute. Can you tell me the other stars of the show you watch every week, including the night in question?

Byrd: Robert Ulrich, I know, but I don't know who else.

Once again, I allowed the subject to drop but returned to it later in the cross-examination. I asked him to summarize the plot of the *S.W.A.T.* episode he saw, and he did so in a vague way.

Me: Just so the jury is clear, you're saying that on the night of the shooting, you were home with your wife and your kids, and you were watching *S.W.A.T.*, which you do every week.

Byrd: Yes.

Me: That is not correct, is it, Mr. Byrd? Because the truth is that *S.W.A.T.* was not on that night.

Byrd: I'm telling the truth.

Me: Isn't it a fact that the show was preempted by the movie *In the Heat of the Night*?

Byrd: No.

Me: Your Honor, I have a *TV Guide* that I would like marked for identification. I'd like to show *TV Guide* to the witness.

Judge Scott: Proceed.

I showed Byrd the listing. He stared at it for a long minute, then put the magazine down in his lap, totally deflated.

Me: *S.W.A.T.* was not on that night, was it?

The defendant hung his head.

Byrd: I guess it wasn't.

When Byrd stepped down, Scott leaned over to me in an aside. "I guess you really *S.W.A.T.*-ed him there, didn't you?"

The jury convicted Byrd, and the judge handed down one of his patented "Maximum Scott" heavy sentences.

A few judges delight in puncturing the solemn atmosphere of a courtroom. I remember a Manhattan Supreme Court Justice named Gerald P. Culkin, who became a little loosey-goosey in his last years on the bench. A round-bodied gentleman with a receding hairline, with his quick wit and tough exterior, he resembled a character from a Damon Runyan story.

One late morning, Culkin handled a robbery case that involved two defendants, both of whom had the last name of Rivera. They were accused of attempting to steal a bicycle from a kid who was also named Rivera. The prime witness was the bike owner's mother, Mrs. Rivera, who saw the incident and called the police. The cop who made the arrest was named . . . Rivera.

"Let me get this straight," Culkin said. "The defendants' names are Rivera, the complainant's name is Rivera, the witness's name is Rivera, and the cop's name is Rivera—and I'm going to the Riviera!"

He tossed the case file theatrically into the air, adjourned the case until two o'clock, and left the court for a lunch break.

While many prosecutors held the belief that certain judges were incompetent, they were too smart to express their view out loud. But there were other judges who were both tough and well respected. State Supreme Court Justice Harold Rothwax was one of those. Rothwax would never let anything slide during proceedings before him. Sloppy presentations, repetitious arguments, ill-prepared attorneys—hell hath no fury like Harold Rothwax.

Rothwax had a lot of nicknames. The Prince of Darkness was one I heard often. Media coverage was unrelenting during the trial of Joel Steinberg, a disbarred criminal defense attorney. Rothwax was on the bench for the trial of Joel Steinberg, who was accused in November 1987 of murdering the six-year-old girl he and his wife, Hedda Nussbaum, had illegally adopted.

The numerous tabloid reporters who had assembled for the Steinberg trial had never encountered anyone like the Prince of Darkness. Rothwax's acerbic interruptions of attorneys chilled not only the targets of his anger but everyone else present.

Rothwax wasn't a guy anyone could bullshit. As a young ADA, I tried a case before him involving an individual accused of robbery, who was represented by a well-known defense attorney. A flashy, well-dressed man, the defense attorney seemed to live to piss off

Rothwax. The lawyer couldn't seem to show up in court on time and often came ill-prepared, never ways to make Rothwax happy.

The attorney cross-examined the victim and the chief witness to the robbery, who happened be wearing a long-sleeved shirt on that hot summer day. The attorney badgered the guy, trying to get him to admit that he was at the scene to purchase hard drugs, not marijuana as he'd claimed.

Defense Attorney: Isn't it a fact that you went down there to buy heroin?

Robbery victim: No.

Defense Attorney: Isn't the reason you're wearing long sleeves is because you have track marks on your arm?

Robbery victim: No.

Defense Attorney: Isn't it the fact that you inject heroin subcutaneously?

The robbery victim clearly had no idea what the defense attorney was talking about. Judge Rothwax interjected a helpful clarification.

Rothwax: You know, injecting it into your arm.

Robbery victim: No.

Defense Attorney: Then you wouldn't mind rolling up your sleeves and showing your arms to the jury?

Rothwax asked me what I thought of the suggestion. I shrugged my shoulders.

Me: I have no objection.

The robbery victim rose from the witness box, rolled up his sleeves, and displayed his arms to the jury. His arms looked clean, with no scars or track marks.

Defense Attorney: Let the record reflect that there were needle marks on the arms of the witness.

I rose to my feet.

Me: No, let the record reflect that his arms are clear.

Rothwax: The jury has seen his arms. They'll make their own decision.

Rothwax summoned the defense attorney and me up to the bench. Rothwax habitually employed a sarcastic phrase that he invoked whenever he encountered sloppy behavior on the part of lawyers. "I'm sure you're aware of the dangers of over-preparation." I thought he was going to come out with that line right then and there. Instead, he leaned over and looked the defense attorney right in the eye.

"I thought before you were just dumb," he hissed. "But now I see you're not dumb. You're just stupid. Now step back."

I thought I had a weak case for the prosecution based on the witness's shaky testimony. But the defense attorney managed to snatch defeat from the jaws of victory, losing the respect of both the judge and jury. The defendant was ultimately convicted and sentenced to state prison. The defense attorney was later disbarred for behavior unrelated to this case.

I always wonder if the gladiators in a Roman colosseum respected the lions. In the legal arena, I mostly respected the defense attorneys I faced in court. I've already mentioned that people who are assigned legal aid attorneys often have pretty good representation. In fact, they might have better representation than many of the people who were able to pay their lawyers.

In many trials, the people who could afford lawyers ended up with generalists who did other work besides criminal law. Some of these lawyers tried a case in criminal court once in a blue moon, and they were just not up to the task at hand.

Some of the best defense attorneys in the nation are in New York City. Many of them are former DANY assistants. They are able to utilize their experience as former prosecutors simply because they had served in the office, most of them under Morgenthau. Knowledge of the other side makes them formidable opponents in court. To paraphrase Sun Tzu in *The Art of War*, "Know the enemy and know yourself; in a hundred battles, you will never be defeated."

ADAs look at each case individually, assess the evidence, and determine the strength of the case. Based on that, they decide what plea bargain to offer, when appropriate. A prosecutor who has a strong case often takes a tougher position during plea bargaining. But I've always believed you have to balance toughness with being consistent.

Defendants who commit the same crime and have a similar criminal record should basically receive the same plea offer. In two robbery cases, for example, each defendant might have robbed a bodega with a gun. They both have a similar criminal record. One defendant shouldn't be offered three to nine years, while the other guy gets five to fifteen. Consistency has to be a bedrock value of the law.

I always told ADAs that if defense attorneys requested conferences, they should listen to them. Perhaps the plea offer is off base, or there's overlooked evidence, or an alibi needs to be checked out. My position is that the prosecution is obligated to listen to the defense.

Try as everyone might to eliminate uncertainty, it nonetheless hangs over the justice system, an "x-the-unknown" factor of circumstances that are beyond anyone's control. Some of the uncertainty stems from the judges and lawyers on the case, but a lot of it involves a jury. Everyone in the legal profession knows a fundamental truth: juries can be unpredictable.

If the prosecution breaks a defendant's alibi, that's usually all she wrote. Game over. A discredited alibi should mean a guilty verdict. As I said, that's usually true. But I recall an instance where I broke an alibi and still lost the case.

The charge was attempted murder. The defendant was a drug

dealer who shot someone who owed him money. The defendant put forth his alibi. "I could not have shot him because I wasn't there that night."

Simple and direct, right? But the dealer happened to be under surveillance by the Drug Enforcement Agency (DEA). I provided the jury with photographic evidence that the defendant was indeed in the exact area of the crime during the exact time when the shooting occurred.

The jury came back with an acquittal.

I could not believe it. How could a jury return a verdict of not guilty when I proved that the defendant was a liar? The photo didn't lie! It was time stamped! It proved that he was present at the scene of the shooting.

One of the jurors spoke to me after the verdict. "The victim was so high on cocaine that we didn't trust he could positively identify the defendant as the one who'd shot him. And you had the burden of proving his guilt beyond a reasonable doubt."

Every prosecutor, defense attorney, and judge has a similar story. The proposition "you just never know with a jury" will get a rueful nod in every legal arena in the land.

It's out of anyone's control. Some of these jurors are not truthful, in the sense that they hide their prejudices. Some of them want to be on a jury, and they'll tell you what they think you want to hear during the selection process.

A trial is a search for the truth, and the jury is the trier of the facts. In other words, the jury will listen to the evidence, determine the facts, and apply it to the law as given to them by the judge. The goal is to select a fair and balanced jury to listen to the case. However, both the prosecutor and the defense attorney will try to select jurors who they feel will be more sympathetic to their side. Prosecutors look for conservative jurors. Prosecutors like to have law-and-order types who tend to support the police and find their testimony credible on their jury. On the defense side, they look for the opposite: social workers, actors, musicians, and liberal and creative folks who are more likely to conjure up a reasonable doubt.

I remember one case where I ran out of preemptory challenges and ended up getting stuck with a social worker juror. I said to myself, "I'm going to get screwed! I have a social worker on the jury!"

The jury came back with a conviction. Afterward the jurors were dismissed, the social worker passed by my table. He must have been stricken from so many juries on the grounds that he was a social worker.

"You see?" he said. "Social workers can convict."

Yes, they can, and dice can roll repeated straight sevens. But I would still seek to play the odds.

CHAPTER 10

A MURDER IN CHELSEA

Though it was late in the day, foot traffic still crowded the busy sidewalks in Manhattan's Chelsea neighborhood on Wednesday, October 31, 1979, a Halloween evening in New York City with fair skies and no rain. The streets were swarming with costumed characters. No one noticed the three-man crew who entered the eighteen-story French-Gothic edifice known as the Industrial Building at 150 W. 28th Street.

The trio crossed the stylish lobby and took the elevator to the sixteenth floor. One of the men had visited two weeks before, casing the premises of room 1604, Mar-Den Creations, Inc., a jewelry design workshop that specialized in diamond settings.

Real-life ghouls rather than holiday ghosts, the three waited in the hallway for the locked door of the Mar-Den showroom to open. When Ellen Wingo and two other employees ended their workday and exited from the shop, the three gun-wielding intruders pushed them back inside. They announced themselves by firing off a single shot from a handgun, a blank cartridge that sounded huge but harmed no one.

Perhaps the trio had watched a few too many crime movies, because the leader, wearing a brown leather jacket, needlessly stated their intentions. "This is a stick-up!" he shouted, holding a gun to Ellen Wingo's head. "Into the back, now!"

The situation went south in a hurry. Kyriakos Loucas, the shop owner, was sitting behind a desk in the back room. His nephew and partner, John Kikis, stood nearby, both shielded by a Plexiglass barrier.

"Johnny, get your gun and shoot!" yelled Loucas.

Responding to his uncle's command, John Kikis pulled out his licensed .38 caliber revolver and fired two shots. The copper-jacketed bullets crashed through the Plexiglass. Hit twice, the gunman lurched forward and raised his own pistol, firing point-blank at Kyriakos Loucas through the Plexiglass as well. This time the shots weren't blanks. A round hit Loucas in the chest, and he fell dead.

The wounded robber staggered back out to Mar-Den's locked front door. Panic-stricken, he struggled feverishly to force it open. The three would-be thieves finally made their way out into the hallway and bolted down a flight of the nearby fire stairs.

Dripping blood, the wounded killer quickly grew weak, dropping his pistol on the landing a floor below. On the sixth floor, his companions discovered a laundry cart and dumped him into it, then placed another cart on top in a futile attempt to hide the leader of the crew. The deathly pale murder suspect looked as if he was going to die, so his two cohorts fled the scene, leaving him behind, and vanished into the Halloween crowds.

The botched attack, the murder of Kyriakos Loucas, and the frantic, stumbling getaway took all of three minutes. Forty-five minutes later, around six o'clock that evening, an NYPD cop followed the blood trail to discover the comatose killer.

His name was Vasko Guraj, an Albanian immigrant in his early twenties. Nearly dead from loss of blood, taken under armed guard, he was immediately transported across town to Bellevue Hospital.

I happened to be on call that Halloween night in 1979. All the senior ADAs in the bureau rotated on homicide calls, handling whatever murder arrests came in during a twenty-four period. The homicide of Kyriakos Loucas came in, and the case against Vasko Guraj sparked my interest. Typically as Deputy Bureau Chief, I would have handed it off to an ADA. Not this time.

The judge lined up for the Guraj case was Burton B. Roberts, well known for controlling his trials with an iron hand. He suffered no fools. He was a bit of a charmer with a booming voice he did not hesitate to use. Prosecutors and defense attorneys coming before him understood they had to be on their toes. He enjoyed schooling everyone in the courtroom on the finer points of the law. Knowing that this case would come before Judge Roberts, I resembled a batter offering to go up against an all-star pitcher.

From both my own experience, and by reputation, I knew Burt Roberts to be a tough customer on the bench. He would become famous—or infamous, depending on your point of view—as the real-life model for Judge Myron Kavitsky in Tom Wolfe's best-selling novel, *The Bonfire of the Vanities*. Morgan Freeman would play the character (renamed Leonard White) in the 1990 film adaptation.

I actually relished the chance to act as prosecuting counsel in Judge Roberts's courtroom. If you have full confidence in your game, you want to play against the best, because it's the only way to test how good you are. When it came to presenting in court, I was experienced enough to gauge my strengths and weaknesses, pluses and minuses. One thing I had was a great memory. My strong suits were cross-examination and especially summations—the summing up of the elements of a case before the jury retires to deliberate.

I always worked hard on my summations, writing them out by hand, rehearsing them until I had them cold. I had a summation almost fully memorized after the second or third read-through. With practice, the words transformed into eidetic imagery, and

I could see them in my mind's eye. I still might have some note cards in front of me, but I rarely referred to them.

During my summations, I simply sought to have a conversation with the jury—a one-sided conversation but with a casual, direct, story-telling kind of style. I looked jurors in the eye. I didn't have to keep going back to my notes.

We convened the Guraj homicide trial in Manhattan Supreme Court at the end of June 1980, eight months after the shooting death of Kyriakos Loucas in his shop at Mar-Den Creations. I was assisted by Richard Kaye, a young ADA. Judge Roberts was present and very much in presiding mode. He had been an assistant district attorney in the Manhattan DA's office and afterwards served as the Bronx District Attorney, so he still had something of a prosecutorial mindset.

The trial took a full six weeks and turned out to be one of the highlights of my professional career. Roberts was a ballbuster throughout, bellowing and yelling whenever he felt the need. He constantly tossed out queries and questions, interrupting at any point, and offering up random legal wisdom of his own—all of which tended to derail my train of thought when I was presenting.

It was as if Roberts enjoyed cat-and-mouse toying with attorneys, ruthlessly killing whatever momentum they sought to maintain. He might have been convinced he knew my job better than I did, an attitude I had occasion to experience even before the jury was fully empaneled.

During *voir dire*—the process where jurors are chosen from the jury pool—both the prosecution and defense can preemptively reject a prospective juror without stating a cause. But such challenges were limited, and I had just about run out of my quota. I decided to accept a woman whom I might not have taken if I had my full quota, but I was still fairly comfortable having her on the jury.

Roberts beckoned me to approach, staring down at me from the bench. He held a yellow legal pad over his mouth to shield his words from the jury.

"You asshole! Are you fucking out of your mind? You're taking her? She's a nut!"

All I could do was stand my ground. "We'll see at the end of the trial if she's a nut or not."

I put all the witnesses on the stand who had been present at the scene, as well as a witness who was working late at a neighboring office that evening and heard the commotion in room 1604. He testified that he poked his head out into the hall and saw a man matching Guraj's description run past him heading toward the fire stairs.

I brought into court the Plexiglass partition behind which Kikis stood and Lucas sat, and had a glass expert testify as to the path of the bullets that were fired based on the convex or concave shape of the holes. I also brought in a blood-splatter expert to explain what the stains at the scene implied. I had an analysis done on Guraj's blood so I could match the sample from the accused with the blood trail on the floor. I called a ballistics expert, the medical examiner, and other witnesses.

Guraj put up an alibi defense. He said he had taken a bus down from Forty-Seventh Street to Twenty-Eighth, showing up at Mar-Den because he wanted to get a diamond ring appraised. He swore he was an innocent man, one who inadvertently stumbled in on an armed robbery in progress and got caught in the crossfire.

As lame as it is, the "I just happened by" defense is a common defense strategy, invoked regularly by the guilty since time immemorial. It seldom worked, and I wasn't about to let it pass unchallenged this time.

After six weeks of trial and dozens of exhibits placed into evidence, William L. Jacobs, Guraj's attorney, gave his summation, and I presented my own. I had done my usual preparation, writing out what I wanted to say, reviewing it time and time again to make sure it indeed said what I wanted it to say. The summation was my chance to lay out how I saw the case and to convince the jurors to see things the way I did concerning the events that occurred at Mar-Den Creations that evening in Chelsea.

Attempting to convince a dozen people of any proposition is difficult. Try getting a handful of friends to settle on the choice of a restaurant for lunch. Or how about you and your spouse agreeing on what color of car to buy? But unanimous agreement is exactly what the justice system demands. It is what the incredibly complex exercise of mounting a jury trial seeks to accomplish.

"Ladies and gentlemen," I began, "the law allows me, the Assistant District Attorney in charge of the presentation of this case, the opportunity and the privilege of summing up the evidence on behalf of the People. A summation consists of the arguments of counsel based upon the evidence that has been adduced at this trial. During the course of my summation, I'm going to attempt to advance arguments to you based upon common sense, logic, and reasoning.

"I cannot go into the jury room with you as the thirteenth juror. But I can give you something to take with you into that jury room, which are my arguments based upon the evidence in this case. I am not going to repeat what every witness said. However, I would ask that each and every one of you join me now to analyze the evidence, and to hold up that evidence, to scrutinize it, and determine what actually happened on the evening of October 31, 1979.

"You've listened to Mr. Jacobs's summation. With his arguments, ladies and gentlemen, what he has endeavored to do is to basically cloud the only two issues in this case, and those two issues are:

"One: Did Vasko Guraj enter Mar-Den Creations, room 1604, on the evening of October 31, 1979, with the intent to rob the premises and Kyriakos Loucas? And, secondly, did Vasko, in fact, shoot and cause the death of Kyriakos Loucas? Those are the issues in this case. They are the only issues in this case."

I was just hitting my stride when I was treated to one of Judge Roberts's patented interruptions.

"Shoot Kyriakos Loucas to death in the course of and in furtherance of the robbery, or in the immediate flight therefrom?" he asked unnecessarily. "Is that correct, Counsel?"

I tried not to display any hint of annoyance. "That is correct, Your Honor."

I went on to point out that the People's case based itself on circumstantial evidence. None of the witnesses testified conclusively that it was Vasko Guraj who broke into Mar-Den and murdered Kyriakos Loucas. The scene was too chaotic and brief for those present to make a clear statement to that effect.

"Each of the witnesses in this case possesses certain facts. The facts that those witnesses present to you are the pieces of the puzzle. As the final piece of that puzzle fits in, you will see that Vasko Guraj was the person, along with two others, who broke into room 1604 and shot Kyriakos Loucas on October 31, 1979."

Easily understandable metaphors, such as "pieces of the puzzle," represent vital elements of a summation. I wanted the jurors to grasp what I was saying, not get lost in flights of rhetoric. I tried to paint a picture of the terror of the moment. I felt that I had told the story of the crime in a way that was solidly based on the evidence and testimony provided. That's what a summation often is: a story, a narrative—this happened, then this happened.

Here is why we know that this occurred, and this, and this. All that was left to say was a sober reminder of the juror's oath.

"Ladies and gentlemen, you have assumed an important responsibility, and I ask you not to take this lightly and to be true to yourselves and to the oaths that you took as jurors. Remember, in accepting your oath, you promised the Court and you gave me your assurance that you would not let any issues of sympathy, emotion, or punishment enter into your deliberations, and that you would decide this case solely on the evidence that you received.

"If the defendant committed the acts charged in the indictment, and that has been proved beyond a reasonable doubt—and I submit that it has—he should be sanctioned by you, ladies and gentlemen, the voice of the community. He should be found guilty of the crimes charged in this indictment.

"I asked each and every one when you were selected as jurors about whether you might feel uncomfortable passing judgment on someone, and whether you might feel that you may have to use reasonable doubt as a subterfuge from performing a task that is not a happy task—in fact, passing judgment on someone and finding him guilty is an unpleasant task. You gave me your assurances you could pass a guilty judgment.

"Ladies and gentlemen, I now hold you to that task. I ask you in the name of the People of the State of New York, and in the interest of justice, to find the defendant Vasko Guraj guilty of the crimes charged. Thank you."

I sat back down at the prosecutor's table, only to have Judge Roberts call me up to the bench after the jury retired to decide their verdict.

"That was one hell of a summation you gave," he said. This from a jurist who gave out compliments as if each good word he doled out would cost him a year off his life.

Roberts must have been at least somewhat right about the effectiveness of my summation because the jury came back quickly, deliberating less than an hour, unheard of after a six-week murder trial. They convicted Vasko Guraj for the murder of Kyriakos Loucas. True to the code of honor among thieves, Guraj never gave up the names of his accomplices, who in the eyes of the law were just as guilty as he was. Somewhere out there, a couple of murderers have never paid for their crimes.

I approached Judge Roberts after the jury was dismissed and the courtroom cleared. Recalling his warning at the beginning of the trial about me choosing to seat a juror he thought was "nuts," I had to get the last word.

"So much for that crazy juror, I guess, right?"

For one of the few times in the trial, Roberts remained silent.

Press conference at DEA headquarters in New York City following the seizure of 1500 kilos of cocaine from a boat named Phoenix by the New York DEA Task Force. Standing left to right are Assistant District Attorney Kevin Suttlehan; Bob Bryden, Special Agent in Charge of the New York DEA Office; Robert Silbering; New York City Police Commissioner Bill Bratton; and Major Bill DeBlock of the New York State Police.

Page 1 headline in the New York Daily News on July 6, 1978 announcing the arrest of two suspects in the Hugh McEvoy murder case.

Robert Silbering and New York Governor George Pataki.

Robert Silbering and Harrison Ford on the set of the movie *Presumed Innocent*.

United States Attorney General Janet Reno and Robert Silbering.

Robert Silbering and New York City Mayor Rudy Guiliani at City Hall in 1997.

New York City Police Commissioner Ray Kelly and Robert Silbering.

New York City Police Commissioner Howard Safir presenting Robert Silbering with an award at his retirement dinner on December 2, 1997.

District Attorney Robert Morgenthau and Robert Silbering.

Sterling Johnson with his trademark nightstick walking on the streets of New York City with Robert Silbering in 1997.

Press conference in Morgenthau's office. Seated left to right are New York City Police Commissioner Bill Bratton, District Attorney Morgenthau, and Robert Silbering.

Bob – you are the best!   Bridget

Three Special Narcotics Prosecutors: Robert Silbering, Bridget Brennan, and Sterling Johnson.

Proclamation presented to Robert Silbering by the New York City Council.

Drug Enforcement Administrator Tom Constantine speaking at the retirement dinner for Robert Silbering on December 2, 1997 at the New York Athletic Club. From left to right are Robert Morgenthau, Bridget Brennan, Tom Constantine, Robert Silbering, and Peter Kougasian.

Press conference dealing with the forfeiture of the Kenmore Hotel.

THE DISTRICT ATTORNEY
COUNTY OF NEW YORK

March 16, 1998

Dear Bob:

Thank you very much for your gracious letter of resignation. I appreciate the fine and wonderful sentiments expressed in it about your association with our office and your kind comments about me personally. I am delighted to learn that you found the experience both memorable and challenging.

We are sorry to see you leave, and we will miss your extraordinary ability, your sense of justice and fairness and your keen humor.

You have had a remarkable career in both the District Attorney's Office and in Special Narcotics. Every responsibility you have undertaken was done in a professional manner commencing with your prosecution of the Willie Bosket case. As Deputy Bureau Chief of Trial Bureau 30 you quickly assumed administrative responsibilities which prepared you for the positions of Bureau Chief of Trial Bureau 60, Chief Assistant of SNC and Special Narcotics Prosecutor for the City of New York. In addition, you have been a great role model and teacher for our young Assistants.

I am deeply grateful to you for redefining the office of Special Narcotics and implementing innovative and creative ideas which have been an inspiration for other offices in the country. As a result of your leadership, Special Narcotics prosecutes more drug cases and writes more search warrants than any District Attorney's Office in the country.

It has been a pleasure having you on the staff from both a legal and personal standpoint, and I will always appreciate your loyalty and your friendship.

The high regard in which you are held by all of our associates testifies to your outstanding qualities of character and personality. Your many friends and former colleagues join me in extending our best wishes to you and our hope that your new association will be a source of great satisfaction to you and that you will enjoy continued success, good health and happiness.

Sincerely,

Robert M. Morgenthau

Mr. Robert H. Silbering

Morgenthau letter responding to Robert Silbering's letter of resignation.

Official photo of Robert Silbering as the New York City Special Narcotics Prosecutor.

3/12/97

N.Y. Daily News 3/12/97

Feds in Queens snatch 2-ton cocaine shipment

By MIGUEL GARCILAZO
Daily News Staff Writer

In one of the biggest drug busts in city history, authorities seized a tractor-trailer in Queens that contained 2 tons of high-quality cocaine hidden amid 30 tons of carrots.

The Colombian cocaine, worth an estimated $100 million, was sealed in plastic shrink-wrap, secreted in a 4-by-4-foot box and camouflaged by the carrots, said Robert Silbering, the city's special narcotics prosecutor.

The truck bore Texas plates and was on its way to a Queens safe house when it was grabbed by authorities in Corona over the weekend.

The dope was intended for distribution to Washington Heights and other parts of the city, officials said.

"It took a five-hour search to locate the drugs amidst the 60,000 pounds of carrots," said Silbering, adding, "In addition to the cocaine, investigators also seized $1.3 million in narcotics proceeds from an apartment in Corona, Queens."

The seizure was the culmination of a seven-month investigation by the federal Drug Enforcement Administration and the New York Drug Enforcement Task Force.

Nine people were arrested,

including 39-year-old Geraldo Gonzalez, who is believed to be the mastermind behind the smuggling scheme, investigators charge.

"He also arranged for sales of smaller quantities of cocaine to traffickers in the New York metropolitan area," said Silbering.

Gonzalez, one of four suspects charged with conspiracy and first-degree drug sales, faces a mandatory minimum sentence of 15 years to life in prison if convicted.

The 3-foot-tall pile of cocaine sat on display at the DEA's office near Manhattan's meat-packing district yester-

day along with big bundles of $100 bills.

Silbering refused to reveal the exact location of the bust because the case is being heard by a grand jury.

The Gonzalez drug ring apparently has suffered two recent, additional setbacks as federal agents seized large sums of cocaine and cash and arrested several alleged drug smugglers in the organization.

On Feb. 25, DEA agents raided a Corona, Queens, home near the Grand Central Parkway at 110th St. and seized 345 pounds of uncut cocaine concealed in produce crates.

A second raid, two days lat-

er, turned up 235 pounds of cocaine stashed in the trunk of a livery cab in the Bronx.

The New York metropolitan area is a major drug distribution point and seizures of large amounts of narcotics are not uncommon.

In 1993, detectives raided a Rego Park, Queens, warehouse and seized more than 850 pounds of cocaine with a street value of at least $40 million.

And in 1991, federal drug agents scored the biggest drug bust in state history when they seized 5 tons of cocaine hidden in the hull of a fishing boat off Long Island.

DEA, DRUGS, DOLLARS: Drug Enforcement Administration officials display 2 tons of seized cocaine and $1.3 million in cash seized over weekend.

DAVID HANDSCHUH DAILY NEWS

March 12, 1997 article in the New York Daily News on the seizure of two tons of cocaine in Queens, New York. It was the largest seizure of narcotics in New York City history.

Press conference with city and federal officials dealing with the forfeiture of an apartment building in Washington Heights that was involved in drug activity for a number of years.

CHAPTER 11

BUREAU CHIEF

n 1984, Bob Seewald, my longtime mentor at DANY, was then Bureau Chief of Trial Bureau 60. As Morgenthau often did, he worked to secure a judgeship for a worthy assistant prosecutor on his staff, helping to elevate Seewald to a judgeship on the Bronx County Criminal Court. Just as people say about nature, bureaucracy also abhors a vacuum. Because Seewald was moving on, it meant the bureau chief slot would become vacant.

I was still Deputy Bureau Chief in Trial Bureau 30. Rubie Mages was Seewald's deputy at 60. She had a year or two more experience at DANY than I did. As a matter of course, she considered herself an obvious choice for promotion to head Trial Bureau 60.

But Morgenthau had other ideas and summoned me to his office a few days before Seewald departed.

"I'm going to promote you to go to 60 and replace Bob Seewald," Morgenthau said. I wasn't given much of a choice in the matter. That was pretty much the whole conversation. It wasn't a discussion, but I certainly was more than willing to accept the promotion.

I thought I knew where the notion of me getting the job originated. Bob Seewald might have put in a good word for me, but I sensed another hand behind the scenes.

Jessica de Grazia functioned officially as the office's First Assistant District Attorney but unofficially as Morgenthau's consigliere. She was very bright and always told you exactly what she thought, which I think is why Morgenthau valued her counsel. If someone was going to be the one to put a bug in the Boss's ear, it would be the plain-talking, tough-as-nails de Grazia.

A Yale Law School graduate, always a big advocate for people she considered worthy, de Grazia was a prime example of the formidable women Morgenthau mentored in the formerly all-male domain of DANY. She was respected by most but also disliked by quite a few.

De Grazia wore many hats in the DA's office, but most importantly, she served as Morgenthau's sounding board and confidante. She was one of the only people I knew who regularly addressed him as "Bob." I was astonished once to witness her chewing out the Boss after he put in a poor showing at a press conference.

"What the fuck were you thinking?" Jessica yelled at him. More surprising than that, Morgenthau simply sat there and took it. He even apologized!

The combination of Bob Seewald and Jessica de Grazia effectively swayed the Boss. Though it was Morgenthau's decision all along, he was an effective administrator in that he knew the wisdom of listening to others. We might think that the law involves only statutes and briefs and dusty libraries stocked with heavy tomes, but the truth is that the law is a people business, and that human interaction is alive and well in the halls of justice.

That may be why I prospered in my professional career. I am a people person. In 1981, after a little over seven years at DANY, I could trace my path from an intern, to a hired-fired-and rehired Assistant District Attorney, to moving over to Family Court and creating the Juvenile Offense Bureau, and to my days as a Deputy Bureau Chief in Trial Bureau 30.

Now I would be awarded a trial bureau of my own.

It wasn't exactly a meteoric rise, but it was steady. In my mind,

I pictured DANY as a mountain, with my friends and colleagues climbing upward or falling off. If you screwed up, your ascent came to sudden stop. Robert Morgenthau stood at the summit like a wise Indian swami, surveying the scramble below him, picking out those he would move up the mountain and those he would divert. This or that person might be lured away to go into private practice. A judgeship might siphon off others.

Was the struggle upward a Darwinian case of survival of the fittest? Perhaps, in the abstract, but it didn't feel like that in practice. No one had the long knives out, looking to stab others in the back. Rather, we were, by and large, collegial and friendly, a band of brothers and sisters.

The transition from Deputy Bureau Chief at 30 to Bureau Chief at 60 felt fairly effortless. As the number-two man in the bureau, the deputy chief deals with the day-to-day operations, while the bureau chief sets the tone on how the bureau is going to run. The final arbiter—the final decision maker—is the bureau chief. He or she has the ultimate word, with the deputy bureau chief working alongside him, almost like Captain Kirk and Mr. Spock.

Since I had worked as a deputy bureau chief, I understood the functions of the bureau chief once I got to 60, so there wasn't a steep learning curve involved. I hit the ground running from the start. At least partly, to the extent that I could, I modeled myself after Bob Seewald, who knew how to foster a smooth, effective work environment.

I always tell people that there are many different types of managerial styles. You have the George Steinbrenner type, where employees succeed because they are afraid to fail, since they know they will be fired if they fail. Morgenthau represented an iconic figure, like Zeus on Mount Olympus or Moses on Mount Sinai. They are revered and respected, but tend not to socialize with their staffers, and they don't tell you very much about their personal lives. They're very businesslike. There's another type of boss who's standoffish, doesn't show much emotion, and is hard to read. They are neither respected nor revered. They're all business and are just interested in getting the work done. These bosses keep their distance, don't socialize, and, as a result, don't motivate their troops.

Then there are bosses like me, friendly schmoozers who give people pats on the back, joke with them, and make them feel valued and respected. I was blessed with the ability to get along with people and evaluate the strengths and weaknesses of the people I worked with. I also knew that each person needed to be dealt with fairly and respectfully. I treated the people I supervised like family, joking with them, and complimenting them that they were the best. I never got much sleep, but I always kidded people that it was time for my nap. Even Morgenthau once called me in the afternoon and asked me if I was awake. To this day, people will call me and ask if I'm awake or if it's time for my nap. Oftentimes, I will end a conversation by saying it's time for my midday nap so I can wake up rested for lunch. People love it. Friends at work will look at their watches and end a lunch meeting, saying that it's getting close to my three o'clock afternoon nap.

The assistants knew that I was easy-going and approachable. Perhaps this is why my ADAs were so loyal to me. Each assistant felt important and like a valued member of the team. They knew that my door was always open, and they could come in and discuss a case or a personal matter. I never raised my voice to the staff or got angry, but they never confused my kindness with weakness. I could be tough when I needed to be, especially in court when dealing with defense attorneys or judges. Even juries seemed to like me because they saw a down-to-earth prosecutor just doing his job of presenting a case and making arguments to them based on the evidence.

I promoted and encouraged people, gave them important tasks, and helped them to succeed. One of the reasons my staff worked hard was that they wanted to demonstrate that my confidence in them was well placed. I found I could do simple things that would mean a lot. When I was Bureau Chief and we got a conviction on a big case, it was bagels for everyone!

My time as Bureau Chief proved to be the happiest period that I had at DANY. One of the reasons for that was the atmosphere around the bureau felt like a family. We all got along very well. Everything just seemed to mesh. The bureau had good metrics, meaning we were successful in getting convictions in the majority of cases we took to trial. We managed everything from misdemeanor cases, such as pick-pocketing and disorderly conduct cases, all the way up the ladder to homicides.

I had thirty-five ADAs working under me in the bureau, many of whom were excellent trial attorneys. Senior Trial Attorney Myles H. Malman actually started with me as a trial preparation assistant and then became a leading trial lawyer at Bureau 60.

One of the numerous homicide cases that Malman tried was a double murder investigation that came to us from New Jersey, which fell under DANY's jurisdiction because one of the killings occurred in Manhattan.

At the bureau, we nicknamed the case "Divorce, Hoboken Style" after the city where the two twenty-five-year-old defendants lived. Hoboken has always had something of a mob presence and was the birthplace of Frank Sinatra (not that there's any connection between those two facts). Stephen Azzolini, a contractor, and Dennis Raso, a florist, conspired to kill each other's wives. The two men hatched the plan for the first murder while drinking together in a Hoboken bar in March 1978.

The plot resembled the Alfred Hitchcock movie, *Strangers on a Train*—although in this case, the two conspirators weren't strangers but childhood friends. In exchange for a partnership in Raso's florist business in Hoboken and a payment of $1,500, Azzolini agreed to kill Raso's wife.

That summer, Rosa Raso had her throat slashed in Manhattan. A month later, Mary Ellen Azzolini, seven months pregnant, was shot in the head in her Hoboken apartment on Washington Street.

After the first murder, Azzollini returned home to New Jersey, where his pregnant wife, Mary Ellen, saw his bloody clothes and asked what had happened. Azzollini told her that Raso had killed his wife and that he had helped dispose of her body. Mary Ellen threatened to contact the police. After discussing the threat with Raso, the two men devised a plan to murder Mary Ellen. While Azzollini visited a friend in North Bergen to establish an alibi, Raso shot and killed Azzolini's wife.

It took a while for the complicated investigation to sort itself out, and the case didn't go to trial until the fall of 1981.

At the trial, Malman called cooperating witness, Dennis Raso, to the stand and asked a rather dramatic question: "Did you enter into a conspiracy to murder your wife?"

"Yes," Dennis Raso answered simply and directly. The jury was visibly shocked at this admission and remained spellbound for the remainder of Raso's testimony. Raso had turned on Azzolini, his co-conspirator, and pleaded guilty to being involved in both killings.

The co-conspirators were both convicted, with Stephen Azzolini receiving two concurrent life sentences—one in New York and one in New Jersey—while cooperating witness Dennis Raso pleaded guilty to a charge of second degree murder and was sentenced to 15 years to life.

Myles Malman was something of a character. He was always well dressed, smoked a big cigar, and had a flair for the finer things in life. He invited me to attend his third wedding. I called him up to tell him that I had a scheduling conflict.

"I can't make this one, Myles, but I'll come to the next one." He laughed good-naturedly.

Myles then went on to a stellar career, becoming the Chief Assistant in the United States Attorney's Office for the Southern District of Florida.

We kept in touch after he left DANY. In the late 1980s, I fielded a call from Malman. "You'll never guess where I am," he teased. Since the news during that period was full of the invasion of Panama, I could well have guessed, but I played along.

"I'm in Panama," Malman said, a tone of glee in his voice. "We just found Noriega."

Manuel Antonio Noriega Moreno, the former strongman leader of Panama, had been indicted two years before by a Miami grand jury on racketeering, money laundering, and drug charges. He had been on the run from U.S. forces, employing lookalikes and other stratagems to throw pursuers off his trail, and finally claiming sanctuary in the Vatican's embassy in Panama City. This was the infamous instance of the U.S. Army besieging Noriega's hide-out, blasting a Van Halen rock-and-roll recording at him until he surrendered. Noriega was subsequently brought back to the States to be tried and convicted by Malman and his team.

Who could ever claim a prosecutor's life is uneventful?

The press is known as the Fourth Estate, a term dating from the French Revolution (the other "estates" were the clergy, the nobility, and the commoners). In other parts of Europe, the media is alternately referred to as the "fourth power."

In my job as a prosecutor, I sometimes considered the press to be a fifth wheel, an additional and unnecessarily intrusive aspect of my job. But newspapers, television, and assorted media indeed represented a powerful force that I could not afford to ignore.

Whenever a prominent case brought on media attention, the ripples spread throughout the office. Not only were local reporters looking over our shoulders at DANY, but sometimes national journalists. The larger the headlines, the bigger the interest on the part of the brass. So media coverage brought in the eighth floor (where the DANY executive offices were), and at times even Albany or Washington, DC.

I learned this firsthand during the Bosket case, when Peter Zimroth made it clear that periodic updates were required. If a story appears in the tabloids, there's suddenly a voice from the front office on the phone: "Where are we going with this? What's happening with this case? Let us know where it's headed, okay?" As Bureau Chief, I might assign a specific assistant to such cases, such as a senior ADA who was media savvy, or someone who understood that there were people in and out of the office monitoring a trial's progress.

More than once, I told my assistants that if a notorious case went south, they'd be seeing their faces on the front page of the tabloids—or worse, my face, or worse still, Morgenthau's. The scandal-mongering *New York Post* particularly represented a Sword of Damocles hanging over our heads. Woe to any ADA who botched a major case and brought Rupert Murdoch's minions down upon our heads.

DANY's public information office organized a press conference for every major conviction and every criminal trial that held the media's interest. I suppose it could be said that it was part of community outreach, but it was really a way to ensure the voice of the prosecution would be heard. Of course, defense attorneys interacted with the press all the time, and some of them were expert media manipulators. The District Attorney's office had to be heard to balance out the picture that the media was presenting to the public.

Manhattan has always been famous for ferocious media attention and high-profile trials. In my era, the Bernard Goetz "Subway Vigilante" case triggered a veritable press frenzy, as did the Robert Chambers's "rough sex" killing in Central Park, as well as the very troubled Central Park jogger case, and the assassination of John Lennon. This was the golden age of tabloid murders. Who could forget the classic *New York Post* headline: "Headless Body in Topless Bar"?

I had solid working relations with the reporters from TV and the print media. No one ever did a hatchet job on me or on any case that we handled. We were really pretty lucky. I always tried to be straight with the press while still keeping sensitive information about cases firmly under wraps. I'm not sure if the principle of honesty applied the other way, to the "ink-stained wretches," as they called themselves, in the media.

I remember one reporter who covered Manhattan Criminal Court for the *New York Post* for decades. I read one of the articles he had written about a case I handled when I was in the Supreme Court Bureau. I could not believe what I was seeing. I called him up at the newspaper.

"I read what you quoted me as saying, and I didn't say that!"

"I know," he responded. "But what I wrote was better."

The tabloids had a rule of thumb, summed up in the phrase, "If it bleeds, it leads." But murder wasn't always a requirement for bringing down the press hordes. At times, the simple notoriety of a defendant was enough.

In the mid-1980s, Mark Gastineau, a New York Jets defensive

end, gained a ferocious reputation on the football field as one of the game's finest pass rushers, a leading member of the vaunted "New York Sack Exchange." At six foot five and two hundred seventy pounds, Gastineau had an outsize, flamboyant status off the field, too, and was highly visible on the Manhattan nightlife scene.

In September 1983, Gastineau and the rookie Jets quarterback Ken O'Brien got into an altercation at Studio 54. The nightclub gained fame for its decadent extravagance, including stunts such as dumping four tons of glitter on the dance floor so New Year's Eve celebrants would be "standing on stardust." For the media attention they garnered, pro athletes were always the darlings of the New York City clubs, though occasionally that notoriety could backfire.

The tabloid response plotted out the altercation as if it were the equivalent of a World War II battle. Gastineau and O'Brien were subsequently arrested on misdemeanor assault charges. When the case fell to Trial Bureau 60 for adjudication, I assigned a sure-handed, highly competent ADA named Jeffrey Schlanger.

Schlanger acted as the trial lawyer, but I was the one who ended up handling Gastineau's pre-trial interview that his lawyer had requested to give Gastineau's side of the story, and proclaim his innocence. This was a strategic decision on my part. If Schlanger had interviewed him, he wouldn't be able to try the case because he might have to appear as a witness, as I subsequently had to at the trial.

Jurors found Ken O'Brien not guilty, but Schlanger convicted Gastineau on assault charges. Because of the large number of witnesses and lengthy cross-examinations, the trial ballooned into one of the longest misdemeanor trials in recent city history, lasting three and a half weeks.

CHAPTER 12

SPECIAL NARCOTICS

In early October 1984, Robert Morgenthau again requested my presence in his office. By this time, I had experienced more face-time with the Boss, so this kind of summons wasn't as anxiety-inducing as it was when I was a newbie rising through the ranks. But it was still a source of slight unease to walk down the hallway of the eighth floor toward the man's office.

Luckily, Ida Van Lindt was there to soothe my nerves. We had developed a bantering back and forth whenever we met. Trying to keep things light, I used to greet her as "my little turtledove," the kind of joking nicety that probably wouldn't fly nowadays. But she knew I thought she was terrific and the turtledove business was simply a friendly term of endearment. One evening when we met at an official function, the annual Hogan-Morgenthau Alumni Dinner, I greeted Ida with a simple "hello there." She responded with mock dismay. "What, no 'little turtledove' this time?" We laughed and hugged.

When I met with the Boss this time around, as usual, he didn't mince words, jumping right into the subject at hand.

"I've got a big problem with Special Narcotics right now," he said. "There's a lot happening down there, but I can't get any status reports from them. I'm in the dark here."

By "Special Narcotics," I knew he was referring to a troubled entity more formally called the Office of the Special Narcotics Prosecutor for the City Of New York. The New York State legislature created SNP in 1971, officially empowering it to address the free flow of narcotics across county lines. The Special Narcotics Prosecutor is chosen by the five county District Attorneys. Francis Joseph "Frank" Rogers, another Bronx boy like me, was appointed as the first Special Narcotics Prosecutor in January 1972. Sterling Johnson succeeded Rogers, and he was head of SNP for sixteen years before his appointment as a federal judge.

Known by the shorthand abbreviation of "SNP," for Special Narcotics Prosecutor, or "SNC," for Special Narcotics Courts, the office had the authority to investigate and prosecute felony cases involving narcotics and other related crimes.

New York City stands unique in its division into five separate boroughs, each with its own district attorney empowered to prosecute crimes committed there. The city has also long been a major hub of international narcotics importation. Each drug shipment might have a single point of entry through one of the five boroughs but may wind up distributed to all.

For all its storied history and independent organizational structure, I knew SNP currently had something of a bad reputation. It was like Devil's Island; no one wanted to be relegated there. For Morgenthau, who lived and died by statistics and information, he wasn't getting what he wanted and the situation had gone code red. Its citywide jurisdiction created many of its problems. District attorneys from the Bronx, Brooklyn, Queens, and Staten Island often used Special Narcotics as a dumping ground for ADAs, transferring their bottom of the barrel, worst of the worst, least capable—or maybe just least popular—assistants there.

ADAs had to be dragged, virtually kicking and screaming upon being assigned to the place. Most such transfers considered SNP as a dead-end career killer. But some of the outer county ADAs turned out to be solid, especially those assigned there during my tenure at SNP. One such ADA was Alan Tomaselli, a Bronx transfer, who became a respected trial bureau chief.

Morgenthau wasn't interested in talking about SNP's reputation, but he did care about its overall efficiency. "I have to do something," he told me. "What do you think we should do?"

I felt honored that he used "we," as if the Boss and I were co-conspirators and he was coming to me for my sage advice. But I was a little puzzled as to why he was talking to me about SNP. All I knew about the place had come from second- or third-hand gossip.

"It sounds like you need a disciplinarian in there," I said. I suggested the name of an ADA on the staff who was known as a tough administrator.

Morgenthau shot me down. "I don't think so," he said. "I think they need someone who's got good managerial skills and good people skills." In other words, someone who could work with Special Narcotics Prosecutor Sterling Johnson, the head of the office.

Still a little slow on the uptake, I searched my mind for someone who would fit the bill.

The Boss didn't wait. "What would you think about going over there as Chief Assistant?" he asked. Since SNP handled all of Manhattan's felony drug cases and was staffed overwhelmingly by Manhattan assistants, the Chief Assistant was always selected by the Manhattan District Attorney.

His suggestion seemed to come from nowhere. Me? What had I done to deserve this? I thought I had been doing a great job in Trial Bureau 60. In my own mind, I thought I deserved to be rewarded, and I was certainly stunned about the move to Special Narcotics.

As current head of SNP, Sterling Johnson had ushered the office into the modern era. He succeeded via his extensive network with both local and national law enforcement. Because of his background, he had excellent connections within the NYPD, and since he had spent time liaising with the DEA, he was also well-respected by agents there. He served as the face of SNP, traveling all over the globe to give presentations on narcotics interdiction, heading to Albany and Washington, DC, to ensure the office maintained a high profile, nationally and internationally.

A problem arose because somebody had to watch the store while Sterling worked his world-wide network. That job naturally fell to his Chief Assistant, a perfectly capable fellow named Charles Joseph Heffernan, whom everybody called Chuck. Sterling Johnson and Chuck Heffernan worked at a high professional level when they were apart. Together, they were oil and water.

When Morgenthau offered me the Chief Assistant position at Special Narcotics, replacing Heffernan, Johnson and Heffernan had essentially stopped talking to each other. Neither one trusted the other. There were over seventy ADAs working cases in the Office of the Special Narcotics Prosecutor, and they were split into two camps: Sterling partisans and Heffernan partisans. The situation had become untenable. No wonder none of the other assistant prosecutors in the DA's office wanted anything to do with the place.

"The assistants who are there aren't happy," Morgenthau told me. "It's reached the boiling point where something has to be done. The office has become dysfunctional."

A problem, yes, but was I the one to solve it?

I thought I knew where this idea was coming from. Jessica de Grazia functioned as the power behind Morgenthau's throne. Jessica had been one of the people who had recommended me for the top spot at Trial Bureau 60. So it made sense she would bring my name up for SNP.

"First of all, Boss, I'm very happy where I am," I told Morgenthau. And I was. As I've mentioned, I considered my role as Bureau Chief at Trial Bureau 60 to be one of the high-water marks of my professional career.

I should have stopped there, but I didn't. "Second of all," I went on, "I don't know the first thing about narcotics cases. I never tried one, never had anything to do with that area of the law. And I don't know anything about Special Narcotics either."

"Well, why don't you go home and think about it?" Morgenthau suggested. "If you decide you don't want to go, I will under-stand."

I did exactly that. I conferred with my very own brilliant consigliere, my wife Shelley. I told her of my extreme reservations about the new post.

"You know, the place is a shithole," I said. Shelley gave me a look, like *tell me how you really feel.* "No, really, what do I want to go over there for? I'm happy right where I am."

We talked it over. Finally, she came up with a question that decided the matter. "Can you really say no to Morgenthau?"

I tried and failed to picture it in my mind. "Well, you have a point there," I said.

"If you say no to him this time, will he ever ask you to do anything again?"

Shelley convinced me to take the job. It turned out to be one of the best decisions I ever made.

I knew there was trouble at Special Narcotics as soon as I walked through the door. My appointment as Chief Assistant took effect

on October 9, 1984. I felt like a member of the French Foreign
Legion, sent to a troubled command post way out in the desert.
The first person I encountered was a secretary sitting at her desk
in slippers, reading a Harlequin romance novel. Engrossed in her
book, she didn't look up or react to my presence in any way.

"What's going on?" I asked her, realizing the obvious answer
would be "nothing."

"Who are you?" she responded. "What do you want?"

I explained that I had just been appointed Chief Assistant of
the office. The news didn't appear to faze her.

I realized right then that I had my work cut out for me. The
entire office had an air of sleepiness and quiet disorder. Located
on the sixth floor of the state office building at 80 Centre Street,
across the street from 100 Centre, where I had spent most of my
professional life, the actual architecture of the office was grand
enough. Marble floors, mahogany woodworking, a lobby with the
kind of Art Deco touches common in the 1920s, which was when
the place was built.

But impressive surroundings could not guarantee good work
being done. Morgenthau had solved the Heffernan versus Sterling
Johnson "house divided" problem with a staffing reshuffle. Bright
and capable, Chuck Heffernan got moved to a position as Senior
Trial Counsel. I was his replacement as Chief Assistant of SNP.

It took about two weeks for all the arrangements for the
transfer to be made. Before this time, Sterling Johnson and I had
never said one word to each other. Our paths never crossed. I
finally went over and introduced myself to Sterling, and that was
the first time we met.

What could have been a slightly awkward situation turned out
not to be. We had a very congenial, very productive first meeting.
At that time, he had just turned fifty and still had an impressive
physical presence, built like a linebacker. We meshed well even

in that initial get-to-know-you. He proved to be witty, open, wise, and expansive. I felt as though we were going to get along.

I had also done a little homework on the man and came to understand what an astonishing journey he had traveled to get to where he was as the Special Narcotics Prosecutor. He grew up in the Bedford Stuyvesant neighborhood, to the outside world a Brooklyn ghetto known for high crime and downtrodden residents. But when Sterling told stories about his childhood, Bed Stuy came alive as a vibrant community. He credited his background with providing him with a sense of humor, as well as a street-level brand of common sense.

Sterling served in the Marine Corps from 1952 to 1956, afterward joining the NYPD, experiencing plenty of racism in both the military and policing environments. When he joined the NYPD, a Black cop was not allowed to partner in a squad car with a white cop. Among the African American partners Sterling pulled was Ben Ward, the first African American New York City Police Commissioner.

Sterling wasn't the kind of guy who was content to remain a beat cop. He attended Brooklyn College and eventually obtained a law degree the same way I did, and in the same place too— Brooklyn Law School, which he attended at night while he was on the job during the day. He eventually made detective, working the streets in his old neighborhood, then moved up to the Homicide Squad. He gained a deep understanding of the city in a hands-on, boots-on-the-ground kind of way.

Graduating in the top ten percent of his law school class, Sterling passed the bar and was hired as an Assistant U.S. Attorney for the Southern District of New York, an office headed up by Robert Morgenthau. After three years as an AUSA, there came a string of high-profile positions. He headed up the Civilian Complaint Review Board for the NYPD, went to Washington when the Drug

Enforcement Administration was a fairly new organization, and became the Special Assistant to the DEA administrator. As part of that job, he traveled all over the world to gain perspective on the drug trade.

Throughout his rise to the top, Sterling Johnson never lost his street smarts, always retaining his connection to the neighborhood realities of New York City. His trademark nightstick represented the truth of this. Strolling the halls with his baton outside a grand jury room, the Special Narcotics Prosecutor himself was once assailed by two gray-haired ladies wanting directions to the restroom. I witnessed the interaction.

"There's a security guard," I heard one of the ladies say to the other. "Let's ask him where the bathroom is." Forgive them their prejudices, but they saw a big Black guy carrying a nightstick in the corridor of a courthouse—what were they to think?

In public presentations, Sterling spoke off the cuff, without a note or piece of paper in front of him, yet came off as a forceful, confident, charismatic speaker. He proved great at thinking on his feet, expertly giving witty comebacks. During a talk at Harvard Law, he was heckled by a voice from the balcony, shouting out the same question, over and over. "What about justice?" the insistent heckler wanted to know. "What about justice?"

Sterling at first ignored the guy, then cut him off. "You want to know about justice? Justice is a statue in the courtyard that all the pigeons shit on!" The whole audience broke up laughing.

If there were any two entities tailor-made for each other, it was Sterling Johnson and SNP. When Frank Rogers left SNP in 1975, Robert Morgenthau didn't have to look too far for his replacement. Sterling Johnson built SNP into a leader in the field, the first prosecutor's office in the country dedicated strictly to offenses involving illicit drugs. He mounted big cases, busting narcotics traffickers not only on his home turf of New York City, but also in cases that had a nationwide and international impact.

So here was the man I got to know during our first meetings, two New York City kids, an African American from Brooklyn and a Bronx boy with a Jewish background, the chief of SNP and his new assistant. It might not have worked but it did, right from the get-go.

I explained to Sterling that I didn't have that much experience dealing with drug crimes in the city.

"You want to know what's really happening on the streets?" he responded. "You have to get out there and talk to folks, get into the housing projects, hear what they're saying."

He searched among the papers on top of his desk. "I just got another notice about a neighborhood meeting somewhere . . . here it is, Community Board 10, up in Harlem."

If you ever want to witness democracy in full-throated action, attend a community board meeting in New York City. According to the formal charter, a community board's primary mission is "to advise elected officials and government agencies on matters affecting the social welfare of the district." Since this is New York, the word "advise" should be interpreted very broadly, meaning "to let everyone know vocally, loudly, and at times raucously, chapter and verse, just exactly what the hell is bothering you."

In December 1984, I did what Sterling suggested and attended a community board meeting in Harlem. I didn't expect to get much out of it and considered the trip uptown merely as part of doing due diligence on the job. My position demanded periodically taking the temperature of the community I served. I would head up to Harlem, listen to some citizens let off steam, and be home in time for the sports reports on the late local news broadcast.

Destiny had other plans. The board met in the heart of Harlem at the Adam Clayton Powell, Jr. State Office Building on 125th Street. That evening represented the first time I heard a word pronounced—a single slang word that would change everything, sharply altering the trajectory of my professional life, but also tragically impacting the fortunes of the entire country.

Crack.

CHAPTER 13

THE CRACK EPIDEMIC

"What are you going to do about crack?" the woman stood up to ask. "It's getting so that my children can't step out of the door without being bothered by dope dealers." She went on to describe the horrors of a new type of extremely addictive and cheap form of cocaine, which was processed into rock-like crystals and smoked.

Others at the community board meeting in Harlem that evening voiced their agreement. I was sitting in front of the crowd on a panel of city officials, and I kept hearing the same word repeated like a curse.

Crack.

I tried not to appear as baffled as I felt. Someone explained that the word referred to "rock cocaine," but that didn't help me out that much. I was Chief Assistant at Special Narcotics, but I was in the dark about this new development. I recall sitting there thinking, *What the hell are they talking about? What is crack?*

The mention of the drug in that meeting marked the first hint of an avalanche that was already in the process of crashing into New York City. Over the course of the next few months, crack would consume my working days and sleepless nights. It would continue to do so for the next decade. The processed, smokable form of cocaine triggered violent drug wars that challenged law enforcement's ability to respond.

At SNP, we were already well aware of the popularity of

powdered cocaine. Along with heroin and marijuana, the alkaloid derived from the coca plant represented a large part of our concern. By one DEA estimate, sixty-five tons of cocaine entered the country in 1983, smuggled by land, sea, and air across every U.S.border. The market proved incredibly lucrative, with gangs, cartels, and whole armies of dealers ready to take advantage of America's seemingly bottomless appetite for coke.

But powder cocaine remained a rich person's high. A night of even mild consumption of the drug could wind up costing hundreds of dollars. During the 1980s, the economy boomed, so there were many consumers who could afford the relatively high expense. In fact, the drug became an emblem of luxury and privilege, proof that a person had the funds to spare for a thousand-dollar splurge.

Crack was different. A rock of crack cocaine, usually purchased from a street dealer in a small plastic vial or glassine envelope, offered a ten- or fifteen-dollar high. Meanwhile, a dose cost around $2.50 to make, so dealers enjoyed a markup of four hundred percent or more. The effects of the drug kicked in immediately. Here was a dream product for drug dealers: instant gratification at a price that almost anyone could afford.

Smokable coke had actually lurked around the edges of the black market for years. *Basuco,* a paste residue of coca leaf processing, took hold in South American slums during the 1970s, but contained remnants of harmful solvents that limited the appeal in wealthier areas. A recipe to refine powder cocaine with ether circulated widely during the late 1970s, coming to greater public attention when comedian Richard Pryor almost perished in a fiery explosion while "freebasing" the drug in June 1981.

Crack put the finishing touches on the evolution of cocaine from an expensive upper-class party favor to a street drug available to all. The recipe involved boiling a mix of cocaine, water, and baking soda to create solids that were then broken up into pebble-like "rocks" offered for sale. Drop a rock or two into a glass crack pipe, fire it up with a butane lighter, and users experienced a cheap high. "Crack" refers to the crackling sound the substance makes when smoked.

Law enforcement played a game of catch up. Sterling Johnson arranged for a former crack "chef" to come into the office, a man who had an extensive arrest record. A little nervous to be surrounded by an audience of ADAs, he demonstrated the method of how to "cook" powder cocaine into smokable rocks.

The lesson was not lost on me. I realized how easy the process was. Given the ingredients, almost anyone could cook up a batch in the average American kitchen, with no special apparatus required.

We're in trouble, I remember thinking, envisioning dozens, hundreds, thousands, of easily created home manufacturing hubs churning out product. During Prohibition the country experienced "bathtub gin," illegal hooch made in the home. Now we had kitchen crack. The drug became so cheap that the phenomenon of "treys" was unleashed onto the streets of New York: small glassine bags of crack that went for the bargain basement price of three dollars.

The reality struck me anew after a vehicle stop yielded $19 million in illicit drug profits. Police officers simply opened the back of a van under surveillance and there it was, a huge cache of cash. I was accustomed to currency taken from cars or apartments, the illegal gains from drug dealing. That was almost a matter of course in Special Narcotics. But most shocking to me in this instance was the fact that this time the money wasn't in hundreds, as had been usual in the past. The cash was in one-, five-, ten-, and twenty-dollar bills because that's how buyers were paying for crack. The drug was so cheap that no one was buying it with "C-notes," as the street slang had it.

The destruction that crack wreaked upon the city could not be overestimated. Almost unheard of before 1985, the drug cropped up everywhere seemingly overnight, hitting vulnerable individuals and marginalized communities the hardest. Like a rolling plague, drug abuse rose to crisis levels in disparate areas of the country, but struck the Northeast with a staggering blow.

The numbers told the tale, as our caseloads at Special Narcotics headed for the stratosphere. Before crack, the total indictments that the office handled annually registered in the upper two thousand range—around 2,800 indictments in 1983, for example. When the epidemic hit, that number more than doubled. In 1987, SNP processed 6,826 indictments, and in 1990, when the number peaked, we did 7,290.

We were being swamped with cases. We didn't have enough personnel. I went to Morgenthau and begged for additional ADAs to be assigned to Special Narcotics, and also suggested hiring "laterals"—people already admitted to the bar but in private practice.

The flood of arrests came in because the police shifted their focus from heroin and powder cocaine to crack. Three Manhattan neighborhoods were especially "hot," meaning drug dealing had become rampant: the Lower East Side, Central Harlem, and Washington Heights. We conducted surveillance, and I was astounded to see the results: grainy night-time footage of street-side drug supermarkets, with customers standing on block-long lines.

The office had to adjust to the new burdens. The federal government funded an initiative called Operation Pressure Point to address the chaotic situation on the Lower East Side. Narcotics officers flooded the neighborhood in a very effective law enforcement push. Five assistants were assigned to handle the cases generated by Operation Pressure Point. But when I checked the numbers, I realized that these five overwhelmed ADAs were assigned two-thirds of the cases coming into the office.

A section of the law known by the shorthand tag of "180.80" dictated a strict policy. When subjects were arrested, and if they were incarcerated because they couldn't make bail, they either had to be indicted or have a probable cause hearing within seventy-two hours.

But the system had become riddled with choke points. The courts were clogged. The police lab had to verify the evidence taken in the arrests was actually narcotics. The five ADAs assigned to Pressure Point arrests worked as best they could, but the seventy-two-hour window was getting blown left and right. Defendants were entering the system and getting quickly turned back out onto the streets. Revolving door justice.

I warned Sterling Johnson of the situation. "If the press gets wind of drug dealers being released without charges, we're going to see ourselves on the front page of the *New York Post.*"

I did what I could. I realigned the caseloads in the office to spread the Operation Pressure Point arrests around to more ADAs. But I felt like the little Dutch boy plugging holes in the dyke. Of course, I would have liked to take more proactive measures, directing this or that defendant into drug treatment programs instead of incarceration, but there was simply no time. I was dancing as fast as I could, busy reacting to a quickly degenerating situation.

During this period, it seemed that my work at Special Narcotics was crack cocaine, all the time. But once in a while, a distraction would lighten my day. Bill Fordes, a former Special Narcotics

ADA, was a technical advisor for the 1990 film, *Presumed Innocent.*

Based on the best-selling Scott Turow novel, the film became a prestige vehicle in Hollywood, attracting A-list stars such as Harrison Ford, Brian Dennehy, Raul Julia, and Greta Scacchi, with Alan J. Pakula in the director's chair.

Bill Fordes asked me to advise the actors on the inner workings of a DA's office. The cast was doing research to develop an understanding of what a prosecutor does and how a prosecutor's office is run. I met with Ford, Dennehy, and their co-stars—Bradley Whitford, Bonnie Bedelia, Joe Grafasi, Raul Julia, and Paul Winfield—and took some of them around 100 Centre to get the feel of the setting.

Scott Turow wrote novels based on his experience as a lawyer. Because there were a lot of courtroom scenes in the book, they were also included in the film. I spoke to the cast members about the feel of a courtroom, basic stuff such as where and when to stand, how to voice an objection, and how to ask questions on cross-examination. They were there to observe my mannerisms, and I would also counsel them on how to avoid gaffes.

"That wouldn't happen in court," I would tell them when they got up and made a speech instead of asking a question to the witness, or when they would ask a leading question. When the film came out, I noticed they had listened and learned—mostly. Dramatic license is always at play in Hollywood.

I became acquainted with Dennehy, who could not have been more gracious when it came to speaking with office staff and signing autographs. He took pictures with anyone who wanted a photo with him.

I marveled at Dennehy's patience and friendliness. "Brian, it's very nice that you make yourself available to these folks," I told him.

"Where would I be without them?" he answered, a real mensch, if I can apply the term to someone with an Irish background.

I was on set when the production filmed a scene involving a medical examiner, the character named "Painless" Kumagai, performed by Sab Shimono and modeled after famed coroner Thomas Noguchi. On one occasion, I took some of the cast to lunch at Forlini's, treasuring the look I got from Joe Forlini when I trooped in with a crew of recognizable faces.

These were the perks of the job. I gave the cast members something of a graduation ceremony when they finished their research at 100 Centre. The production office gifted me with a *Presumed Innocent* jacket. In the summer of 1990, Shelley and I were invited to the East Coast movie premiere, where we were seated in front of Jackie Kennedy. Linda Fairstein, then head of the sex crimes unit and on her way to becoming a best-selling novelist, tapped me on the shoulder.

"I want to introduce you to someone," Fairstein said.

That's how Shelley and I got to say hello to the former First Lady. When friends asked Shelley afterward what Jackie had been wearing that evening, she replied, "It was Jackie Kennedy! You think I was looking at her dress?"

In the wake of the *Presumed Innocent* experience, I maintained relationships with members of the cast. I got to know Joe Grifasi the best. He is a character actor who had been cast in the role of prosecutor Tommy Molto in the movie.

When Dennehy appeared on Broadway, he would invite Shelley and me backstage. Bradley Whitford, who became a star on the television show *The West Wing,* went on to appear in *A Few Good Men* on Broadway and gave us tickets to the show. When the audience stood up to give Whitford a standing ovation, he gestured and nodded to me from the stage. I saw heads swivel in the audience around me, with people wondering, "Who is this guy?"

I can't say my own head wasn't turned by the brush with celebrity. I became accustomed to actors coming to SNP for research. When Keanu Reeves got cast in *The Devil's Advocate*, he visited the office to pick my brain for his role as a prosecutor. Andy Garcia shadowed me for *Night Falls On Manhattan*. Joe Grifasi introduced me to the writer David Milch, who co-created the popular cop show, *NYPD Blue*, with Steven Bochco. With Morgenthau's approval, I was a script consultant on the hit TV series for a number of episodes.

I was beginning to feel like Hollywood Bob. I took a call from a producer in Los Angeles who said she had heard about our work at Special Narcotics and thought it would serve as a great basis for a television series. She brought a handsome soap opera actor named Michael E. Knight to the office, supposedly with the idea that he would play me on the show.

The gulf between the Michael E. Knight fantasy and the Bob Silbering reality must have been too large because the idea never went anywhere. When the stage lights clicked off and the bold-faced names went back to their fabulous lives, I was always perfectly happy to be the same hail-fellow-well-met I always was around SNP. However, it was a nice break from the stress of dealing with crack cases and all the other problems that I was confronted with on a daily basis. I would have never thought that this street kid from the Bronx would be rubbing elbows with Hollywood's rich and famous.

CHAPTER 14

CRISIS IN WASHINGTON HEIGHTS

B eyond incursions from Hollywood, also breaking up my days were odd and interesting events that I never could have foreseen. At Special Narcotics, there was an ADA assigned from the office of the Brooklyn District Attorney, who was a good trial lawyer and quite an all-around character. A family photo was prominently displayed in his office.

"That's my wife, Sasha," he told me more than once, pointing proudly. "And that's my son." He would tell stories about family vacations, and he always requested time off for the Jewish High Holidays.

One day I took a call from the Brooklyn DA's office. "Are you sitting down?" asked the voice on the other end of the line. It turned out that the ADA I had been working with for years had graduated law school but never passed the bar.

Stunned by the news, I thought about all the cases that were now thrown into doubt because they had been prosecuted by a person who was not credentialed to appear in court. Such a revelation could have a cascade effect, possibly upending convictions and voiding sentences, sending other cases to be retried. I was busy for days assessing the damage and containing the impact.

A few weeks later, I got another call from the same Brooklyn official who had contacted me the first time. "I was going through

the guy's file," he said, referring to the uncredentialed ADA.
"You're not going to believe this."

"What's not to believe?" I asked, my heart sinking.

"He had some reference letters in his file, and it turns out one
was from his sister. You know how he always presented himself
as an observant Jew and needed the High Holidays off and
everything?"

I shook my head, even though the person on the other end of
the line couldn't see me.

"The letter from the sister says her brother is very religious all
right, because he goes to church every Sunday."

I was witnessing a professional life disappear down the tubes.
The man's whole existence appeared to be a charade. The framed
portrait on his desk was a ruse. He was leading a double life, to the
degree that he illegally practiced law at the highest level for years.
Thank goodness none of his convictions ended up being reversed
because of his lack of a law license.

Also distracting from the usual office routine was the fact
that the Boss might toss me a curve ball every so often. In 1990,
I received a summons to Morgenthau's office, where I met Peter
Malkin, a Polish-born former Mossad agent. I was vaguely familiar
with Malkin's incredible story about how he was part of the team
that captured Adolph Eichmann, the monstrous mastermind of
the Holocaust, in Argentina in 1960. Of course, I felt that honor
must be paid to this famed Nazi hunter, but I was baffled why the
Boss summoned me to meet him.

Morgenthau had become close to Israeli government figures
at that time, including being friendly with Ariel Sharon, a former
Israeli general and future Prime Minister of Israel. The Israeli
security apparatus helped DANY get information to make
certain cases, and Morgenthau appreciated that. While he was
not a religious Jew, he had a strong sense of Jewish identity.

Later, he would become one of the movers and shakers behind the establishment of the Museum of Jewish Heritage: A Living Memorial to the Holocaust, in Lower Manhattan.

Malkin didn't exactly strike me as a ferocious Nazi hunter. At that time, he looked his age, around sixty years old, a short guy, well-built and balding. I thought to myself, *He looks like a Jewish grandfather! This was the man who took down the architect of the Final Solution?*

That day in Morgenthau's office, there was another individual—a friend of Malkin's—who was under investigation by the office of the U.S. Attorney in New Jersey. Malkin thought he could help his friend by making a deal with Special Narcotics and Morgenthau.

"We have a plan, Bob," Malkin said to me. "We will kidnap someone who is a major, major drug dealer in South America. We'll throw him on a helicopter and bring him to New York so Special Narcotics can prosecute him."

In return for this service, DANY would reach out to the U.S. Attorney in New Jersey, who was breathing down the neck of Malkin's friend, to try to get them to stop the investigation.

I realized this wasn't just a simple meet-and-greet with Peter Malkin. I had been summoned there for a reason.

"Boss," I said, "I don't think this is a very good idea. First of all, there's no indictment against this guy. That's number one. Number two, how is this going to look? Do we really want to get into the kidnapping business?"

Morgenthau nodded sagely. Malkin and his protege looked uncomfortable.

"I think it's a bad proposition all around," I added, sounding a definitive note. "We should just scrap it."

Of course, we never put the plan into motion. I understood that Morgenthau did not want to say no to Peter Malkin directly, to refuse this hero of the Jewish people. Therefore, he brought me in, knowing what I was going to say. I served as his cat's paw. I put the *kibosh* on what was clearly an insane idea so the Boss wouldn't have to. I didn't mind. In fact, I left the office that day again impressed with Morgenthau's shrewdness in handling the matter.

There were no hard feelings. Peter and I eventually developed a friendship. He would call on me for simple favors—introductions and such—and he actually helped us get information on some of our investigations. Peter died in 2005 at the age of seventy-seven. At the time of this writing, the gloves he wore to subdue Eichmann are in Israel and are scheduled to be moved to a newly created exhibit at Yad Vashem, Israel's official memorial to the victims of the Holocaust.

Another example of how Morgenthau dealt with people and situations occurred in 1989. Out of the blue, I fielded a request from John Matthews, a figure in the Long Island Democratic establishment. He suggested that I run for District Attorney of Nassau County.

"I'm registered as an Independent," I told him.

"You're a county resident," he responded.

"Well, I also have a family to support. I can't just take a leave of absence from the DA's office without a fallback. You'd have to find me a paying job of some sort."

Matthews answered by mentioning something about a law school professorship.

I told him I was flattered by the offer and that I would consider it. Then I immediately called Morgenthau to run the idea past him. We wound up going to lunch at Forlini's. I explained the unexpected offer.

"If you want a leave of absence, you can have one, that's not a problem," he said.

But I sensed the Boss's hesitation. I knew his M.O.: whenever he believed employees were underperforming or expendable, he would find them a job outside of DANY. But if he believed you were valuable and important, he would not lift a finger to help you move on—unless, of course, it might help him personally or would benefit the office somehow.

"Let me make a few calls. Let me call Cuomo," he said, meaning Mario Cuomo, who was governor of New York at the time. "We have to see if there's any money and support from the party so you can make a credible run."

Ida Van Lindt called me back two days later to say the Boss wanted to see me.

"I don't think you should do it," Morgenthau said bluntly. "There'll be no money from the party, so you don't have the funds to run a campaign. You're going to be a sacrificial lamb."

I knew all along it would be an uphill climb. Nassau County voted Republican as long as I could remember. The incumbent, the Republican Denis Dillon, had held the office for years. On the other hand, he was under mounting criticism, especially due to his staunch Catholic stance and anti-abortion views.

"I think it would be a mistake to run," Morgenthau repeated. "But if you want to do it, I'll of course grant you a leave of absence."

I left his office still thinking it over. I spoke with Shelley about it that night, who told me that it was my decision to make. However, I could tell she was skeptical that I could get elected after I told her what Morgenthau had said to me at lunch. Over the next few weeks, the Boss never wanted to discuss the matter. Every time I would raise the issue, he would change the subject. That was Morgenthau's way. In his mind, he had given his opinion, and that was the end of it.

I took his advice and informed the Nassau County Democrats that I was not interested in running for the position. At Special

Narcotics, I always had enough on my plate without resorting to international kidnapping schemes or sudden, switching-horses-in-midstream career moves. It was the best decision I never made. I stayed at DANY, and two years later, I was offered a career-making promotion.

Of all the drug-infested neighborhoods in the entire country, Washington Heights in Upper Manhattan stood out. Running from 155th Street north to 190th Street, it became crack central, the number one area where residents felt the impact of the epidemic the most. In 1992, the *Associated Press* labeled it "the city's most murderous neighborhood."

Two hundred thousand people were crowded into the dense, one-and-one half square mile community. Many of them emigrated from the Dominican Republic, and the vast majority were peaceful, law-abiding citizens who went to work every day and did not deserve the plague of drug dealing that had descended on their streets.

A quick check of a map of New York City reveals the reason for the situation. Washington Heights is something of a crossroads. The George Washington Bridge spans the Hudson River there, connecting New Jersey to New York City. The Cross Bronx Expressway slices through the neighborhood, allowing access from the eastern areas of Connecticut and Westchester County.

Millions of tri-state residents live within a short car ride from Washington Heights, and in the 1980s and 1990s, a small but still significant percentage of those millions hungered for a hit of crack cocaine.

I knew the neighborhood well enough. In fact, during my college years, I passed through it every day on my way to New Jersey, traveling from the George Washington Bridge bus terminal on 178th Street. Twenty years later, when I visited as part of fact-finding tours in my role at Special Narcotics, I didn't recognize the place.

As a kid visiting "Wash Heights," or as a student transiting the area, I had always admired the magnificent pre-war residential buildings that lined the streets, with beautiful two- or three-bedroom apartments. Now landlords had chopped them up into SROs: single-room occupancy lodgings.

During my fact-finding visits to such buildings after they had been raided by the police, I noticed that each bedroom had an enormous lock on the door, an indication of the perilous security situation. Three different families often lived in a three-bedroom space, sharing kitchen and bathroom facilities with each other. In other apartments serving as fronts for drug dealing, my NYPD guides would pry up the floorboards to reveal semi-automatic firearms hidden away. What appeared to be an innocent can of soda in a refrigerator was actually a stash with a false bottom, perfect for hiding drugs or cash.

Washington Heights had become a neighborhood under siege. Double-parked cars on the streets were a tell-tale sign of unchecked drug dealing. I toured a decrepit four-story apartment building, a classic crack house, formerly the site of a drug bazaar that the police had recently busted. Among the unbelievable squalor, glass drug vials still littered the floor. The stench of urine lingered in my nostrils for hours afterwards.

In part due to the high-profile murder of Officer Edward Byrne in 1988, Mayor Ed Koch and the NYPD developed the $116 million TNT program, creating "Tactical Narcotic Teams" that were designed to be the shock troops against drug gangs. TNTs were buy-and-bust operations. They consisted of a squad sergeant, an undercover officer who made the buy, four or five tactical officers to swoop in for the arrest, plus a "ghost"—a plainclothes cop with the vital function of keeping protective watch on his undercover teammate in dangerous situations.

Cases from the TNT initiative began to flood my office. Thousands of new defendants entered the system. But I noticed an odd quirk in the geographic distribution of the arrests. TNT teams were making a lot of cases in Harlem, but there was no increased presence in Washington Heights. I reached out to the Chief of Narcotics for the NYPD. We met over lunch at Forlini's.

"Why is TNT focusing on the Twenty-Third and Twenty-Fifth Precincts?" I asked. The Two-Three and the Two-Five covered specific areas in Central Harlem, while the Thirty-Fourth Precinct was centered in Washington Heights.

The chief was a real decent gentleman, an old-style long-time cop who rose up through the ranks to become a respected commander. He knew his job backward and forward, and knew New York City.

"Well, we're picking up a lot of low-hanging fruit in Harlem," he said. "A lot of easy arrests there."

"I'm not seeing arrests in the Three-Four," I said. "Why wouldn't you go to Wash Heights?"

He looked me straight in the eye and responded with words I'll never forget.

"Keep this between the two of us, Bob," he said. "We've lost Washington Heights. It's not coming back. Maybe in ten or twenty years, with gentrification . . ."

The chief trailed off. He looked miserable, and I didn't blame him. This was a devastating admission from the NYPD's Chief of Narcotics. The police force had essentially ceded control of an entire neighborhood to the drug gangs. Even a heavyweight explosion of TNT wasn't going to blast the dealers out of Washington Heights. Drugs were sold brazenly in the streets there, as well as out of apartment buildings all over the neighborhood.

I thought about Edward Byrne. The entire criminal justice system in New York City, from patrol officers on the beat to the prosecutors in the courts, had sworn the rookie cop's death was going to change things. We were going to crush the bad guys who ordered his killing, and we were going to banish the drug culture that brought it about.

I didn't say it out loud to the chief, but I had an unsettling thought. *Are we surrendering to the drug dealers? Is this just one more losing effort, like Vietnam, where all of our efforts proved in vain? Did Edward Byrne die for nothing?*

As the tidal wave of crack crested in New York City, we always sought to interrupt the supply of illicit substances on the streets. Special Narcotics made major cases working alongside the DEA Task Force and the NYPD. We took down neighborhood dealers, confiscated their supplies, and took their illicit profits from them. Buy-and-bust initiatives kept the pressure up on the legions of criminals who were making life miserable for neighborhoods.

We did the best we could with the resources we had, always trying to get more and better ADAs for Special Narcotics. I knew it was imperative to address the flood of cases. The judges themselves were under tremendous pressure because the courtrooms were inundated with buy-and-bust cases. The courts couldn't handle the load.

The situation kept me up at night, the same question repeating itself in my mind: *How the hell are we going to deal with this?* I recognized that I had a real problem on my hands. I finally came up with an idea, and Sterling gave the okay to put it into effect. We had a single large grand jury room where we ran all the Special Narcotics cases. I brought in the carpenters and divided the room in half, splitting it in two, so that we'd have two grand juries in the morning and two in the afternoon.

We also made other changes, such as trimming down the

Special Narcotics trial bureaus from five to three and relabeling them 30-40, 50-60, and 70-80. Each trial bureau was staffed with a bureau chief, a deputy bureau chief, and about twenty ADAs. The streamlined reorganization helped align the office with the three intake parts of the state Supreme Court, which allowed the cases to move more smoothly through the system.

Such measures helped, but they didn't go far enough. The problem was that no matter how many local dealers we took out of circulation, the flow of drugs just kept coming. I realized that we could not simply arrest our way out of the crisis. We had to come up with better, smarter, and more effective strategies. We were slicing off small pieces of the tail of the snake. We needed to cut off the head of the snake by going after and eviscerating the major drug organizations.

CHAPTER 15

MR. SPECIAL PROSECUTOR

The decades around the turn of the millennium might be called the golden era for local district attorneys. New York City was very lucky in this respect. Morgenthau was in office from 1975 to 2009. Richard Brown in Queens was there for almost thirty years. Charles Hynes was Brooklyn DA for a long tenure. Likewise, William L. Murphy in Staten Island, and Robert Johnson in the Bronx, both in office for many years.

I believe continuity is essential for an effective DA's office. In NYC, we were blessed in terms of both the tenure of the local district attorneys and their abilities. Coincidentally, Morgenthau, Hynes, and Brown all died in 2019.

In an interesting side note, the DA of neighboring Westchester County at that time was a tough prosecutor named Jeanine Pirro, who later became a judge and a Fox News personality.

The police commissioners I worked with in my years at DANY and Special Narcotics were less long-term. By and large I had excellent relations with Ray Kelly, Bill Bratton, and Howard Safir, who were in office as police commissioners during my years at Special Narcotics. The relationship between the SNP and the NYPD is absolutely vital. The police need prosecutors to handle their arrests and investigative matters, while prosecutors need cops to provide solid, by-the-book cases and arrests in order to build cases that won't fall apart at trial.

Bratton was the most effective police commissioner I have

worked with. Brought in by then Mayor Rudy Giuliani, Bratton instituted the innovative "broken windows" theory of policing, targeting minor crimes as a way to keep neighborhoods safe and prevent urban decay.

Bratton mounted various other new initiatives, including CompStat (short for "computer statistics"), which employed the power of technology to identify high-crime areas and provide strategic management data. The program placed more responsibility on NYPD precinct commanders to address problem hot spots. CompStat proved so successful in New York that many police departments across the country copied it and started similar programs of their own.

Under Bratton's leadership, the crime rate fell to historic lows, starting in the mid-nineties and continuing for the next twenty-five years, until the trend reversed recently. Unfortunately, Giuliani became envious of Bratton's high-profile success. Plain and simple, Guiliani wanted more credit. It was a marriage destined for divorce. Bratton might have had an expansive ego, but Giuliani had a bigger one. Bratton had to go.

In September 1991, Sterling Johnson was appointed as a federal district court judge for the Eastern District of New York. Such a position represented the crowning achievement of his remarkable career.

Sterling's judgeship prompted a natural question: Who would replace him at SNP? This being New York City, there were some politics involved. A few folks tossed their hats in the ring, formally or informally. Although the newspapers basically came out and labeled me the heir apparent, Sterling himself made a decision to refrain from endorsing me.

"It's not my call," Sterling declared. "It's up to the five county DAs."

Morgenthau was behind me, and he was the key. I knew I could count on the support of the other county DAs. I still had to do a little politicking. In the end, I was appointed Special Narcotics Prosecutor by a unanimous vote of the District Attorneys from Manhattan, Queens, Brooklyn, Staten Island, and the Bronx.

I took over SNP in September 1991 on an interim basis and was formally named head in January 1992. As the newly minted Special Narcotics Prosecutor, I took up the reins of an office of roughly ninety hardworking attorneys who were always on the verge of being overwhelmed by what was happening out on the streets. We were battling an epidemic of narcotics that was eating away at the fabric of city life. Since 1987, the murder rate exceeded two thousand cases every year, many of them drug related.

I felt an all-hands-on-deck sense of urgency. We had to attack the situation in any way we legally could. I embarked on a campaign to employ a host of novel methods to combat the continued assault of illicit drugs on the streets and neighborhoods of New York City. There's more than one way to skin a cat, and I wanted to put that wisdom into play.

Jessica de Grazia promised that Morgenthau would give me the people I needed to build SNP up. After Jessica left the office to move to London with her family, Barbara Jones, a former federal prosecutor, succeeded her and was named Chief Assistant. Barbara continued Jessica's practice of sending solid DANY assistants to Special Narcotics. Barbara was also extremely helpful when it came to dealing with the politics of the other DA's offices. She was later appointed a federal judge by Bill Clinton.

I came to rely on two long-term assistants to help me run Special Narcotics. One was Art Diamond, who ran the Trial Division and knew everything about the flow of cases and how the office operated. The other was Lou Halpern, an Executive Assistant ADA who worked exclusively with the Special Investigations Bureau (SIB) at SNP and was the expert authority on wiretaps.

Morgenthau recruited many capable assistants from the private sector, so-called lateral hires. Dan Donovan is a prime example of the success of this practice. Donovan came to SNP as a lateral and later went on to become Staten Island District Attorney and a U.S. Congressman.

Several other ADAs fortified the office and made it a much stronger place to work. Eric Pomerantz, the man who confronted Willie Bosket when he came looking for me in Family Court, became my Counsel. Eric was very bright, an excellent investigator and trial attorney, and offered sage advice on how to handle a variety of issues. He excelled there before going on to a successful career in the private sector as a legal expert in the healthcare field.

Other members of the executive staff included Jose Maldonado, who became my Chief Assistant. Maldonado gave up a high-paying private sector job with a major law firm to do public service work. He was hired by Morgenthau and sent directly to SNP, where he eventually worked on major investigations. Jose was street smart, loyal, and able to run the day-to-day operations of the office. He is presently the head of the Criminal Division in the New York State Attorney General's Office.

Arlette Hernes, also smart and experienced, remained an Executive Assistant ADA, a position that she held during Sterling's tenure. Rhonda Ferdinand headed up our Alternatives to Incarceration Unit, one of the first in the country. She was devoted to determining which defendants should be given a second chance and avoid prison. She has been honored numerous times for her work in this area.

Matthew Menchel had the important job of Director of Training, a position for which he was well suited. Matt was a student of trial work and loved teaching the assistants how to become better lawyers, giving them tips on how to effectively try a case. At the time of this writing, he is in private practice and one of the most respected trial lawyers in the country.

Both Eric and Matt had misgivings about being moved to Special Narcotics by Jessica DeGrazia in her efforts to build up the office. To this day, they recall how much they learned and enjoyed their time at SNP.

Another standout, and an all-around office favorite, was Peter Kougasian, a gentle, caring, and extremely charismatic man. He came to Special Narcotics as a Bureau Chief in 1996 and stayed at SNP in one capacity or another for over two decades. I knew him well from his previous work at DANY, where he was well respected and well liked. Peter was an excellent writer. Morgenthau would rely on him to help pen opinion pieces for the press. A talented amateur magician, Peter used to entertain us in off hours with witty and impressive routines. I even got him to perform magic tricks at my son's Bar Mitzvah.

Around 100 Centre, Peter was a dynamo, mentoring rookie ADAs, forming deep and enduring friendships with those who worked alongside him. Sonia Sotomayor, a Princeton University and Yale Law School classmate of Peter's, served with him as an ADA at DANY before becoming a federal judge and later a U.S. Supreme Court Justice.

Long after I left SNP, Peter handled one of the most important and impactful prosecutions in the legal struggle against the opioid epidemic. He brought charges of reckless manslaughter against Dr. Stan Li, who ran a pain management clinic in Flushing, Queens, that was nothing more than a prescription mill. As lead counsel, Kougasian secured a game-changing guilty verdict. It was the first time in New York State that a physician faced homicide charges for patient overdoses, establishing a legal precedent for other cases.

Peter Kougasian died in September 2021 after a debilitating

battle with ALS. Some people just seem more alive than others, and Peter was one of those, which made his passing all the more heartbreaking. The outpouring of love and grief when he died brought to mind Shakespeare's line: "Nothing in his life became him like the leaving of it," though in reality there were many, many aspects of this man's life that were remarkable. Not every person on the planet receives a personal eulogy from a sitting U.S. Supreme Court Justice, but Peter did when Sotomayor memorialized him as "a man of integrity, honor, and valor."

A number of SNP assistants later became judges in the state criminal and supreme courts. A few also became federal judges. So many ADAs at SNP went on to other stellar careers, which speaks to the quality of the personnel I worked with.

What made Special Narcotics special? Very simply, the people. As head of the office, I received most of the accolades when we took down a drug organization or gained a conviction in a big trial. But the people I worked alongside of in SNP were like the engine of a ship—they kept the office moving forward and provided the fuel for success. The support staff, the investigators, the paralegals, clerks, secretaries, finance people, and grand jury reporters all played essential roles in keeping the case flow moving and the office afloat.

The attorneys at SNP worked hard to ensure that justice was done, trying to make the communities of the city safer and free of the scourge of drugs. The executive staff, bureau chiefs, and deputy bureau chiefs managed the day-to-day operations of the legal personnel and made important decisions on how cases should be prosecuted. And finally, the men and women of the DEA, NYPD, New York State Police, and all the other law enforcement agencies that supported Special Narcotics deserve recognition for their dedication and tireless efforts to keep New York City and the nation safer.

Special Narcotics had come a long way from being an office that people looked at with skepticism and a place where no one wanted to work. It rose to become the most respected and effective drug prosecution office in the country, one that was relied on for information, advice, and knowledge about the drug trade and the prosecution of drug cases. It was one that ADAs were now eager to join and take part in the investigation and prosecution of major drug offenders. There was always competition among the city's DAs to land the biggest cases and to get as much funding as possible from the city, state, and federal government to run their offices and hire new ADAs. Special Narcotics gave whatever forfeiture it received from the federal government and the state to the five DA offices under a formula that gave the biggest share to Morgenthau.

Focused on money laundering cases, the Eldorado Task Force operated out of the customs offices at the JFK airport. The sprawling five-thousand-acre shipping and transport beehive was located within the borders of the borough of Queens. But if any county DA's office had people working there with the task force, that office would receive a share of forfeiture assets. Because JFK was an international airport, with many flights coming in from Europe, Asia, and South America, this often involved money confiscated from passengers involved in narcotics cases. The amount could easily average millions of dollars per year.

Special Narcotics had investigators working with the Eldorado Task Force, so we received our share of the confiscated assets, which we then distributed to the five county DAs. Judge Brown, the Queens DA, didn't like the idea of any other prosecutor's office working on his turf in Queens. He would have preferred that Special Narcotics remove itself from his bailiwick.

Brown had his Chief Assistant, Barry Schwartz, set up a luncheon in a conference room at the Queens County DA's office.

The arrangement was very official. Everyone at the meeting had a nameplate in front of them. I had a suspicion of how the proceedings were going to go down.

"The Eldorado Task Force works out of Kennedy Airport, which is part of Queens," began Schwartz, telling me what I already knew. "So we are wondering, should you really be out there?"

The gathering brought to mind an old adage about a poker game: If you look around the table and don't see the sucker, then you're the sucker. My job, as I understood it, was not to let them make me into a sucker. I wasn't going to give an inch.

"Look, at Special Narcotics, I work for the five county DAs of New York City," I said. "If three of them want me to leave JFK, I'm gone tomorrow."

They weren't going to give up easily. Schwartz reported back to Brown, and they called me back into Brown's office. Brown sat behind his desk while he allowed Barry Schwartz to do the talking. Judge Brown was short, under five feet tall, and usually let his underlings get involved in the heavy lifting. We repeated the same routine. "We want you to leave JFK to us," Schwartz insisted, raising his voice. Judge Brown sat tight, silent as a garden gnome.

"Barry, Judge Brown, you're both smart guys," I said. "You realize I'm actually doing you a favor by staying. If I leave JFK tomorrow, do you think Morgenthau will just roll over? Does that sound like Robert Morgenthau to you? He will send investigators to work with the task force. And after him will come Hynes and Johnson, the Brooklyn and Bronx DAs."

Judge Brown finally broke his silence, slamming his fist on the desk. "I play tennis with David Dinkins," he barked, referring to the New York City mayor at the time. "And I play tennis with the budget director, Phil Michael. All this money goes to Morgenthau, and the Queens office gets peanuts!"

I shrugged my shoulders. "Judge, with all due respect, I think you're playing tennis with the wrong people." In response, Judge Brown threw me out of his office.

And that was that. The division of the spoils at Kennedy Airport remained the same.

I felt as though I had enough difficulties handling the day-to-day crisis in the streets of New York City without worrying about Judge Brown's bruised ego.

One aspect of Special Narcotics that I particularly enjoyed was the innovative spirit that the assistants brought to the job. An ADA named Chris Marzuk is just one example of someone who was able to pioneer new legal approaches while working at SNP.

Private property has always been a core concept of the legal system, and rules of ownership have been established in common law since the time of Hammurabi. So when we moved to seize the big single-room-occupancy "apartment hotel" on West 165th Street in Washington Heights—a building notorious for drug activity—I knew to step carefully. We were wielding the immense power of the state against private landlords, and such an action could not be embarked upon lightly.

But the recent numbers had told the tale. Even back when I served as Chief Assistant in Special Narcotics, I knew that building was deeply troubled. Between October 1988 and May 1991, the NYPD conducted twenty-three separate searches within the building, turning up thirty-seven pounds of cocaine in thirty different apartments, seizing scales, drug paraphernalia, guns, and cash, and also arresting fifty-five people for narcotics offenses.

Cops found dealers operating in more than thirty of the building's 216 apartments. Surveillance revealed they stored the drugs in the rear of the building. Lookouts posted themselves on the sidewalk in front, and customers placed their orders there, with runners ducking inside to bring back the goods.

We continued to monitor the Washington Heights situation when I became Special Narcotics Prosecutor. I knew the landlords there had been warned again and again. Chris Marzuk, working with Anne Rudman from DANY's Forfeiture Unit and assistants from the U.S. Attorney's Office for the Southern District of New York, used a 1984 law that allowed the seizure of premises used for trafficking in narcotics. Accompanied by an NYPD lieutenant, Marzuk met with the building's executive manager and the managing partner of the corporation that owned the building to discuss the situation. Little progress was made.

More searches resulted in more seizures of cocaine, weapons, and paraphernalia related to the production of crack. An NYPD undercover operation revealed a criminal enterprise run by Euclides Lantigua. On August 5, 1992, officers seized twenty-two pounds of cocaine from Lantigua's apartment and arrested three of his associates. On September 16, 1992, officers searched three apartments used by Lantigua's organization, seized paraphernalia, drug records, and $13,000 in cash, and arrested three more of Lantigua's associates and Lantigua himself.

The evidence obtained in the undercover investigation showed that Lantigua controlled as many as ten apartments in the building, and that the building manager not only knew of Lantigua's drug business, but had also permitted one of Lantigua's associates to rent two more apartments under a false name.

Finally, the other shoe dropped. On October 23, 1992, the United States Marshals Service seized the building. At the time of the seizure, the NYPD executed search warrants in seventeen apartments and seized a total of five pounds of cocaine, a loaded weapon, scales, paraphernalia, and $2,000 in cash.

"Las autoridades federales ocupan un edificio que funcionaba

como foco de venta de drogas," read the front-page headline in New York's Spanish newspaper, *El Diario*: "Federal authorities occupy a building that was used as a focus for the sale of drugs." Acting in concert with the NYPD and the U.S. Attorney's Office of the Southern District, Special Narcotics successfully removed a blight on a Washington Heights neighborhood that had troubled residents for so long.

We had pulled the rug out from under Euclides Lantigua and his cohorts—or, actually, we pulled the floor out from under the rug too. Federal asset forfeiture law is normally aimed at the bank accounts, yachts, and cars of narcotics traffickers. Marzuk and the others forged a different use of the law, targeting the premises rather than the dealers who were operating out of it. Our purpose was to help protect the neighborhood and warn other landlords about allowing their buildings to be used by drug dealers.

The landlords challenged the legality of the forfeiture, and the case went all the way to the United States Supreme Court, where the strategy was vindicated. A *New York Times* writer visited the former crack house a year after the building was seized. "Today the drug dealers are gone," he wrote. "The aging building is peaceful once again for tenants who had endured years of intimidation."[2]

By 1994, buoyed by our success, we employed the same asset forfeiture process to take down another crack house in the tony Gramercy Park neighborhood farther downtown. The Kenmore Hotel stood as New York City's largest single-room occupancy hotel. Under the assault of crack dealers, the place had turned into a horror show, as elderly residents were terrorized and afraid to venture out of their rooms.

---

2 David C. Anderson, "The Editorial Notebook; How to Rescue a Crack House," *The New York Times*, February 8, 1993. https://www.nytimes.com/1993/02/08/opinion/the-editorial-notebook-how-to-rescue-a-crack-house.html (accessed September 24, 2023).

Violence permeated the twenty-three-story red-brick building at 145 East Twenty-Third Street. Alongside drug runners,
prostitutes plied their wares in the unlit hallways. Employees of
the place took bribes to allow customers inside. In the summer
of 1994, an eighty-six-year-old woman was robbed, strangled, and
her dead body left in the bathtub of her room at the Kenmore.
Once again, the building's landlord failed to respond to repeated
warnings about the conditions on the premises.

The late-morning seizure of the Kenmore Hotel on June 8,
1994, came at the end of a series of fruitless negotiations with
the building's owners. At the press conference announcing the
forfeiture, I was joined by Marzuk, who ran the investigation for
SNP, as well as U.S. Attorney for the Southern District Mary Jo
White, and Attorney General Janet Reno.

With the novel strategy of real estate forfeiture, I believed
that Special Narcotics had added another tool to its toolkit. But
I still felt as though we were playing a law enforcement version
of the Whac-A-Mole game. As soon as we attacked one aspect of
the problem, another popped up. Drug trafficking didn't respect
boundaries. If we closed it down in one area, the dealers simply
transferred their operations to another place.

Special Narcotics had the advantage of having citywide
jurisdiction. We could chase down traffickers to wherever they
fled within New York City. But the onslaught of illegal drugs didn't
restrict itself to any one location. It wasn't just a city problem; it
was global.

CHAPTER 16

TASK FORCE

I knew the four necessary elements to make major drug cases: enlisting informants, using undercover operatives to infiltrate criminal organizations, surveillance, and employing wiretaps to gain information about who was bringing illicit drugs into our communities and other critical information about the operations.

Low-level drug dealers—the runners, the cooks, and the street-corner lookouts—were nothing more than interchangeable cogs in the machine. They could easily be replaced by some other young kids who were looking to make quick money. Step by step, point by point, we had to work our way up the organizational levels to confront the heads of the organizations.

In the early nineties, Colombian cartels successfully smuggled between five hundred and eight hundred tons of cocaine a year into the United States. The ultra-violent Medellin cartel, decimated by a concerted attack by law enforcement, gave way to the dominance of the Cali cartel, which was clever enough to hide its criminality behind legitimate businesses. During this time the countries of Central America, especially Nicaragua, Guatemala, and Honduras, had developed into major transshipment hubs for the Colombian cocaine producers.

In October 1994, a tough administrator named Tom Constantine was appointed to the top position at the DEA. Buffalo-born, he had come up through the ranks of the New York

State Police, where he held the position of Superintendent until he was selected for the DEA by the U.S. Attorney General.

I knew Tom for years, and we always had a good relationship. I knew he had his work cut out for him. I went down to Washington to visit Constantine. Whenever he saw me, he always referred to me as "Mr. Special Prosecutor." He began the meeting by quoting numbers, which were trending the right way under his administration. "We're seizing huge shipments of cocaine in Central America," he told me, proudly citing 2.6 metric tons the agency had confiscated in Honduras and 7.6 metric tons in Guatemala.

"Tom, it's great that you seize all this stuff," I said. "But this is a business for the cartels, and losing drugs is just the price of doing business for them. We have to go after the money because that's the key. The cartels are laundering the money and creating businesses to launder the money."

Of course, I was pretty much preaching to the choir. Constantine knew the trafficking business as well as or better than I did. But I was gratified to learn that over the next few years the DEA moved aggressively to attack the financial end of the business. The Agency's "Green Ice" and "Green Ice II" investigations, for example, led to the arrest of the Cali cartel's top financial managers and the seizure of more than $50 million in assets worldwide.

I sought to do more. I loved nailing the moneymen, but the ADAs in SNP sought to proceed up the levels of distribution and go after the head of the snake. In order to dismantle international enterprises, we had to widen the reach of Special Narcotics. To do that, we had to work even more closely with the DEA, which had a global reach.

Bob Bryden and Jim Milford, the local agents in charge of the

DEA's New York City office, helped enormously. Luckily, I was also able to enlist an intrepid judge, Leslie Crocker Snyder, one of the smartest, most effective people that I have ever encountered.

If two organizations were ever a match made in heaven, it was DEA and SNP. The Drug Enforcement Administration held the office of the Special Narcotics Prosecutor in high esteem, and the feeling was mutual. With his strong ties to the agency, Sterling Johnson had cemented the relationship early on. We shared a purpose: the DEA is charged with the enforcement of the Controlled Substances Act as well as investigation of the top levels of domestic and international narcotics traffickers, and that was the goal of Special Narcotics too.

The DEA Task Force, as we always referred to it, really kicked into high gear after Sterling Johnson became Special Narcotics Prosecutor in 1975. Formally called the New York Drug Enforcement Task Force (NYDETF), it is comprised of agents from the DEA, the New York State Police, and the NYPD. It is the best narcotics unit in the country, in my opinion.

The personnel involved were hunting bigger game than neighborhood dealers. They made high-level cases, dismantling criminal organizations not only in New York but nationwide. NYDETF ran complex undercover campaigns that burrowed into the guts of international drug cartels. The DEA agents in the Task Force were not the kind of buttoned-down operatives content with sitting behind a desk. They were larger-than-life figures, some of them treading the fine line between "motivated" and "obsessed."

There's always plenty of publicity about the federal agents of the FBI and the Secret Service. Meanwhile, DEA agents don't get enough credit for the outstanding work that they do and all of their accomplishments. I've always found them to be hard-working, dedicated, and knowledgeable about the drug trade, inside and out. They risk their lives against violent crime cartels, especially the undercover operatives, taking down ruthless drug gangs.

I remember when I first came to Special Narcotics as Chief Assistant DA, and Sterling brought me over to the Task Force to introduce me around. The first agent we ran into was the head of the operation, John Maltz. I looked at this guy and thought to myself, *We must be back in the Old West*! Maltz had a big, bold personality and a look to match: a strapping guy with a bushy mustache, sideburns that ran down his jaw like mutton chops, and wild hair. I thought I was meeting Wild Bill Hickok in person.

"Whenever we need money to make undercover buys," Maltz said with an expansive grin, "I go to Uncle Sterling and Special Narcotics gives us the money, right?"

I didn't catch on right away to all the reasons the Task Force had such an intense appreciation for us at Special Narcotics. I always recalled the phrase "special relationship" that diplomats use to talk about relations between the United Kingdom and the United States. That's what we had with SNP and the DEA Task Force.

Why did the DEA love Special Narcotics so much? Because of Sterling Johnson, of course, and because of the hard work and dedication of the ADAs in SNP. But eventually, the DEA developed a new ally in the fight against violent drug gangs: Judge Leslie Crocker Snyder, a fearless judge with whom agents loved to work. Judge Snyder became our secret weapon in the battle against drug gangs. Snyder was hired by DA Frank Hogan as an assistant district attorney in 1968. She rose in the ranks of the office in an era when you could count the number of female ADAs on the fingers of one hand.

She eventually turned her energies to the way sex crimes were handled, which in those bad old days verged on the medieval. In fact, common law treated rape as a property crime against the husband. Snyder would have none of that, so she embarked on a successful campaign to reform the law, founding and heading up the Sex Crimes Prosecution Bureau, which was the first in the nation. Appalled by how rape victims were being raked over the coals in court, grilled by defense attorneys in ways that sometimes amounted to a second assault, Snyder co-authored a rape shield law that protected them on the witness stand.

In 1983, Mayor Ed Koch selected her for a criminal court judgeship. It was on the bench that I came to appreciate Judge Snyder as a crucial ally. You have to understand that if the agents in the DEA wanted a search warrant or a wiretap, and they were forced to work through channels at their home base of the U.S. Justice Department, the approval process might take a week, two weeks, even longer. The wheels in Washington, DC, turned slowly.

Meanwhile, time was of the essence. Drug dealers had mobile phones, switching networks, and the very latest in electronic gear. Wait a week to get up on a wire, and the phone connection in question had already disappeared, winding up changed or dead.

Judge Snyder came to the rescue. When the DEA wanted a wiretap, it didn't matter if it was late at night or early in the morning, on a weekend or during holidays. The woman was indefatigable. Because of her hard-working attitude, we could be up on a wire in a day or so, sometimes within hours.

It made all the difference in the world. One of the core reasons why the DEA Task Force liked working with Special Narcotics was because we could offer them a quick turnaround on their warrant requests. The agents respected Judge Snyder because she was tough, but they also saw that she understood the pressure of their jobs.

We had a solid working relationship. Beneath her tough, no-

nonsense exterior, Judge Snyder was a friendly and gracious person, with a good sense of humor from her long years working at DANY. She knew the realities of the office very well. She ran a no-nonsense court and handed out tough sentences, but no defense lawyer could ever argue that Judge Snyder didn't know the law.

In specific cases where some alternative to incarceration might be warranted, she would reach out to me (always asking permission from a defendant's attorney) to see if something could be worked out. I'd confer with the ADA handling the case, familiarize myself with the facts of the case, and usually agree with her suggestion.

Judge Snyder wrote of our *ex parte* negotiations in her memoir, *25 to Life*: "Some prosecutors suffer from rigidity and even, sometimes, a lack of guts—unwilling to face down the criticism they think they might incur if they do anything 'outside the box.' Not Silbering."[3]

Judge Snyder definitely represented a silver lining for Special Narcotics, but for every silver lining some people will come up with a dark cloud. I once fielded a call from the AUSA (Assistant United States Attorney) who handled narcotics prosecutions in the office of the U.S. Attorney for the Eastern District of New York, which tried cases in Queens, Brooklyn, Staten Island, and Long Island.

"What the fuck is going on?" he demanded. "Why the hell is the DEA sending you all these cases from Brooklyn and Queens?"

Turf battles between the federal and state prosecutors were usually kept to a minimum. SNP and the AUSAs in the Southern and Eastern districts would huddle and decide where it would be best to prosecute the case. In fact, the levels of cooperation in New

---

3 Leslie Snyder and Tom Shachtman, *25 to Life: The Truth, The Whole Truth, and Nothing But the Truth* (New York, NY: Warmer Books, 2002), 311.

York City were far superior to elsewhere in the country, where squabbles often arose between DA offices or different agencies like the FBI and DEA in the same region.

The circle of trust in New York City extended to the state police, the NYPD, customs enforcement officials, and local offices of the FBI, DEA, ATF, and the Secret Service. As a general rule, we all worked very well together.

But in this instance, the AUSA took a look at the numbers and decided the situation was just too lopsided. He wanted his office to get in on more of the action. He couldn't understand why so many cases that might have gone to the federal courts in the Southern and Eastern Districts were winding up at Special Narcotics instead.

I told the AUSA, "I think there's two main reasons for what's happening. One, I think the DEA agents like working with our ADAs better because they're so much smarter, and two, they're harder working than your attorneys."

I was pulling his chain a little, but it was true—the assistants at Special Narcotics were absolutely tireless in pursuit of drug organizations. I continued on a more serious note, "When the DEA goes to you for a wire, you have to send it through a number of levels at the Department of Justice. You have to wait ten days for an approval, sometimes longer. At Special Narcotics, I can get a wire in twenty-four to forty-eight hours, okay? That's the edge we bring to it. Our warrants, our wires, our people—it's just that simple."

The AUSA replied, "It's Judge Snyder, isn't it?"

What could I tell the man? "Judge Snyder will review the wire application, and when she gives the approval, we're up and running, we're on the wire, we're on the case right away. Those DEA agents are like racehorses. They get skittish if they're made to wait."

Because of the hard work of our assistants and the agents of the DEA, along with the ability to get up on wires quickly, SNP led the nation in the yearly number of narcotics wiretaps approved during my tenure as the head of SNP. It also led the country in the number of narcotics search warrants executed. No other prosecutor's office in the nation came close to handling the number of cases or indictments that the SNP handled. Special Narcotics, without question, had become the country's number-one drug prosecutor's office in the United States.

CHAPTER 17

UNDERCOVER

A s the Special Narcotics Prosecutor, one of my most important roles related to human resources, and making sure the office had the absolute best ADAs, investigators, and staffers that I could possibly find. I hunted down capable personnel as though they were outlaws and I was the new sheriff in town.

Jose Maldonado, my second in command, advocated for the creation of a special unit of investigators made up of retired or soon to retire NYPD detectives. These cops had enormous reserves of knowledge and experience, as well as considerable contacts throughout the city.

"SNP should have its own civilian investigators," Maldonado suggested to me. "The Boss has his group, we should have ours. They can work with the DEA, they could work with the NYPD, and they can make cases."

"That's a really good idea," I responded. Morgenthau had created a cadre of investigators who worked directly with his office. I wish I could say it was my thought to put in place a similar group, but it was Maldonado's all the way.

For the chief of the new unit, we recruited Bill Cook, an NYPD sergeant who had been in the DEA Task Force and retired the year before. Cook seemed to know everybody and was well respected all around.

"We're going to get some more people," I told him. "You know, it reminds me a little of Elliot Ness putting together *The Untouchables.*"

Bruce Meyers had vital technical experience and worked in TARU, which was the NYPD Technical Assistance Response Unit that provided investigative technical equipment and tactical support to all bureaus in the NYPD. Omar Brinkley was a former NYPD cop, savvy and street smart, whom I had worked with over the years on robbery cases. I also enlisted an undercover specialist who had somehow managed to penetrate deep into the Colombian cartels. Bill Cook also helped to bring in a few excellent investigators that he knew and worked with. Within a few months the unit had grown to about a half dozen top-flight experienced investigators, each with their own specialized expertise.

Members of the new unit would pair with a specific ADA to do cases, or partner with NYPD and the DEA Task Force. They teamed up with informants that they had developed while on the job in the past. In addition, they worked cases on their own, because they had the knowledge, the experience, and the relationships to make it work.

Around the office, we started referring to the new group as the "ROD Squad," after the slang term for a pistol, of course, but also as an abbreviation for "retired old detectives." The expertise they had acquired over the years did not simply vanish when they left the police force. We were able to utilize collective decades of experience to make cases for Special Narcotics.

We also stepped boldly into the brave new world of digital communications. As criminals became more sophisticated in their use of technology, SNP and the DEA Task Force followed along. The wiretap room at the DEA's New York field office on the west side of Manhattan was an electronic beehive. Platoons of techs in headphones monitored multiple phone conversations. The Task

Force had wiretaps up on landlines, cell phones, pagers—any of the myriad devices cartels used to carry out their business.

In the 1990's, law enforcement played a high-tech game of cat and mouse. When the drug lords abandoned landlines and took up cellular communications, we were right there with them. Then they dropped pagers in favor of quick-burst computer messaging, and the techs got up on that. Encrypted messages, fiendishly difficult coded language, digital communications—all the latest electronic advances spurred equal and opposite responses in our monitoring efforts.

This state of affairs gave rise to a different form of undercover operation, and a new kind of undercover operative who was as comfortable with technology as with the cops and robbers aspect of the job. First among equals of the new breed was a firebrand NYPD cop from the Bronx. Officer Jerry Speziale's heroic performance during a blazing gunfight brought the brass to the wounded cop's hospital bedside. Mayor Ed Koch and Police Commissioner Patrick Murphy asked Speziale the million dollar question.

"What do you want to do with your career?"

Lying there, recovering from a bullet that tore through his forearm, Speziale could have taken the easy way out. He was a hero. He could have requested any assignment in the world, with a safe and comfortable desk job being the obvious choice. Instead, Speziale went the opposite way, taking the opportunity to sign on to the most dangerous work on the force.

"I wanna be a narc," he said.

There was a method to the man's madness. Working as an undercover narcotics officer offered an accelerated track to gaining the rank of detective, which normally took three to five years. With undercover work, Speziale could be wearing a coveted gold badge much sooner.

And there was something else, too. When the armed robber with whom Speziale had traded gunshots during that Bronx firefight finally went down, the pavement around was littered with glass vials. Speziale remembered thinking, *What the hell is this*? He and his police cohorts had never seen crack before. He had a similar awakening to what I experienced when I first heard the word during that community board hearing in Harlem.

Speziale embarked on a campaign of busting crack houses on the streets of New York City, disguising himself as a junkie, complete with ragged clothing that, for the sake of realism, he smeared with dog feces. Busting local dealers, he got his detective promotion, and in 1989 was assigned to the DEA Task Force.

A New York State Police sergeant named Eddie Beach was the supervisor of Speziale's Task Force group. At the start, the two worked mostly on investigations of traditional organized crime. Beach marveled at Speziale's chameleon-like ability to employ different city accents on undercover jobs.

"He could play a guy from Buffalo and he could play wise guys from Brooklyn," Beach said. "The guy was unreal. He could have been an actor."

The two became friends. Working with a team assembled from the ranks, not only of the New York State Police and the DEA, but from the NYPD as well, they conducted some of most effective undercover operations of all time.

"Everybody in the group had a specific job," Beach recalled. "We had fifteen agents, a couple who were good at undercover work, a couple of people who were good at surveillance. I had everybody doing what they were good at, telling them, 'Everybody doesn't get to go out on the mound and pitch.'"

The law enforcement world consists of a chain, and any weak link along the length lessens the effectiveness of the whole enterprise. Drug cases were first developed outside of court, by agents working the streets, smuggling routes, or haciendas of drug lords. The arrests made there then passed through the hands of prosecutors and judges. The chain passed from law enforcement officers, to the prosecutors, then to the courts.

I devoted myself to ensuring my own realm, Special Narcotics, would never represent a weak link. On the bench, dedicated judges such as Leslie Crocker Snyder held up their end of the chain. But we all depended on the activities of intrepid agents to furnish us with evidence to make good cases. When I try to explain the energy and dedication that these agents brought to their investigations, the word "determined" comes to mind. These people simply refused to let anything stop them.

To give you an indication of the type of expertise Beach, Speziale, and other Task Force agents developed, in the early months of 1996 the group picked up the trail of a major Colombian cocaine producer. His operations generated immense amounts of cash, all of which needed thorough laundering.

Following the old Deep Throat rule from the days of Watergate, the Task Force decided to "follow the money." Beach came to Special Narcotics to discuss the investigation with me, Chief Assistant Bridget Brennan, and the other SIB assistants working on the case. We obtained Judge Snyder's approval for an extensive wiretap surveillance campaign.

To add to his other skills, over the years Speziale had made himself a world-class specialist in cellular communications. He noticed that a target suspect pinged the same cellphone relay station with calls several times every day, a tower on Crooked Hill Road in Brentwood, Long Island.

Since Speziale understood that cell phone signals hit relays in a specific manner, he actually sent an agent to the tower with a compass. Then he followed the direction of the signal to a certain neighborhood. Playing a game of connect-the-dots, he discovered the general area of the stash house where the money was kept.

At 5 p.m the wire room techs reported talk of a money drop to be made the following morning. The money was going to be taken from the stash house and sent down to Florida. But the exact location of the stash house remained a mystery.

"Did they say anything else?" Speziale asked. "Anything at all?"

"Yeah," said the wire room operator. "The guy in the stash house said to pick him up an Egg McMuffin." The order was detailed: no cheese, an orange juice, a medium coffee.

A small clue, but it was the only one Speziale needed. He located a McDonald's within the radius of the cell tower, and had a team quickly set up surveillance on the restaurant that night. An agent was placed inside the McDonald's to let Speziale know when someone gave that specific Egg McMuffin order. Other members of the team set up surveillance in the McDonald's parking lot, and other agents were stationed on nearby roads. No one was getting any sleep any time soon.

Around 8 a.m., a Buick Regal with three men in the car pulled into the McDonald's parking lot. One man got out, entered the restaurant, and put in the specific Egg McMuffin order. The game was now afoot. The agents followed the car to a nearby mansion and set up surveillance. Shortly afterward, the men from the car and someone from the house loaded up the car with boxes containing large cans of Redpack crushed tomatoes. The car drove off, followed by the agents, to a nearby warehouse in Plainview, Long Island. At the warehouse, a garage door opened and a tractor trailer with Florida plates pulled out. The Redpack cans from the car were put on a pallet, and along with thousands of other Redpack crushed tomato cans already on pallets, loaded onto the truck by forklift. The truck left the warehouse on February 27, 1996, headed for Florida, followed by cars manned by the DEA Task Force agents.

Even the most intrepid agent might have tied up the operation there. Bust the warehouse, confiscate the dirty money, call it a day. But Beach and the other Task Force members wanted to take down the money launderers themselves—they were after the head of the snake. Speziale and the team embarked upon a highly dangerous tracking operation that led them through multiple states in a mad rush that, at times, resembled an old-time movie chase.

Speziale and Beach spoke with me and the ADAs handling the case before they put their plan into action. They told us that they had witnessed the transfer of the Redpack crushed tomato cans from the stash house to the trailer, and they were going to follow the tractor trailer to its destination.

"Guys, taking down this tractor trailer is really a good thing," I told them. "I trust you and I like you a lot. But if you're wrong on this, there's going to be a lot of explaining to do. If you're wrong, who is going to pay for the damages?"

Neither Speziale nor Beach responded. I felt like a principal reading the riot act to a couple of misbehaving students.

"You better be right," I said.

Everything depended on the drug money being where the agents believed it was, in the Redpack cans. "I want you to call me every couple of hours. I want to know even if it's two in the morning. Let me know what is in those cans!"

As the truck barreled out of New York and onto the New Jersey Turnpike heading south, the agents tracked it every step of the way. Stuck in my office in Manhattan, getting periodic bulletins, I kept thinking of the O.J. Simpson freeway chase that had gone down only a few months before.

The tractor trailer rig kept running afoul of state troopers along the way in Delaware, Maryland, and Virginia. Meanwhile, it was imperative for the traffickers on the other end of the shipment to believe that everything was okay. The lives of informants embedded in the cartel hung in the balance.

The trip south was not uneventful. Later on, I counted myself thankful I hadn't been in on every nitty-gritty detail. A bleary-eyed Speziale stayed awake for two straight days, putting the plan into action and following the tractor trailer on its interstate journey. He wound up rear-ending a car at a tollbooth. He merely left behind his wrecked DEA wheels and switched to another chase vehicle.

The agents received instructions not to follow the tractor trailer to its final destination in Miami. Arrangements were made for it to be pulled over by local authorities when it crossed into North Carolina from Virginia. Federal agents in North Carolina arranged for an emergency application to a local judge, requesting that the Task Force be empowered to confiscate the suspect vehicle. The North Carolina troopers took the driver in for questioning after they found $15,000 in cash on him that he had been paid to drive the tractor trailer to Miami.

Realizing that they could not continue further south, Speziale and his DEA agent partner, John Sager, climbed into the cab of the tractor trailer. Troopers halted traffic on I-95, and the two executed a U-turn and roared back north.

Several times during the trip north, state troopers with lights and sirens blazing trailed the tractor trailer as it raced through their jurisdictions.

"Virginia State Police actually had the nerve to pull over the trailer," Beach recalled. "We had a certain major down there who wasn't at all happy with my guys. We had a screaming blowout right there on the highway, arguing back and forth. I informed the major that we would arrest him for interfering with a federal investigation."

Virginia state authorities finally allowed the truck to proceed. A sleep deprived Speziale called into Special Narcotics from the road, requesting a search warrant for the contents of the tractor trailer. I figured I had trusted him so far on this case, that I might as well back him all the way. The ADAs involved forwarded the warrant request to Judge Snyder and got her approval.

Finally, after an epic there-and-back-again, multi-state journey, Speziale and Sager pulled into the fenced lot at DEA's headquarters in Manhattan. Quite a reception committee gathered to greet them, including representatives from the U.S. Attorney's office and, of course, Special Narcotics.

I was assailed by doubts. The trail that began with an Egg McMuffin order had led here. I knew that Speziale couldn't be *absolutely certain* that the money from the stash house was on the tractor trailer. Speziale requisitioned a forklift and took every shrink-wrapped pallet out of the trailer. The assembled law enforcement personnel stood staring at 5,500 cans of Redpack crushed tomatoes.

The Task Force brought in drug sniffing dogs. Nothing. They obtained an enormous X-ray machine from U.S. Customs. Technicians ran the cans through the X-ray once, then a second time when the machine turned up nothing.

The group of assembled law officers began to look at Speziale with pity in their eyes, as if a transfer to the Fairbanks, Alaska, DEA office might be in his future. Speziale sent out for dozens of hand-operated can openers and commandeered a nearby dumpster. I kept getting bulletins, batch after batch of tomatoes, opened, dumped, examined, discarded. Nothing was turning up. In a particularly cutting attempt at mockery, a few skeptical DEA agents arranged for a pizza delivery for the crew: two large, no sauce.

Night fell. They had been at it all day. Under floodlights, the scene looked ghoulish, everyone spattered with blood-like crushed tomatoes. Only a few hundred unopened cans remained.

A call went up. "Jerry!" Speziale's partner John Sager yelled. "We got it!"

Some of the last batch of cans contained olives instead of crushed tomatoes. A sealed sandwich bag encased in X-ray proof carbon paper emerged, then another, and another. Each bag contained around $15,000. All in all, $1.8 million in cash was found in the shipment. The bust led to more investigations, more arrests, more confiscations. Beach estimated the total haul of drug dealer cash at over $8 million.

A sense of relief washed over everyone once the money was finally found. The hard work that Speziale and his team put into the case paid off big time. The ADAs who put so much time and effort into working the case were also relieved. I took a deep breath, relieved that I didn't have egg, or rather tomato sauce, on my face and that I didn't have to explain why I gave the okay to open up over five thousand cans filled with crushed tomatoes.

I slept well that night.

CHAPTER 18

SPECIAL INVESTIGATIONS

U nder the heading of "Thrilling Events in My Life I Wouldn't Necessarily Want to Repeat," I'd have to rank pretty much at the top of the list the experience of flying in a wide open Blackhawk helicopter a thousand feet above the jungle of the Dominican Republic. It was like riding in the backseat of a car with no door. I had an uncanny sensation of falling, even though in fact I was buckled in tight.

Election Day 1992, the date voters put William Jefferson Clinton into the White House for the first time, I had landed in Santo Domingo at the invitation of Bob Bryden, SAC of the New York City DEA office. He had organized a fact-finding trip for a group that included Jack Holmes, head of the Organized Crime Control Bureau at the NYPD, and Tom Cash, SAC (Special Agent in Charge) of the Miami DEA office. A local military liaison, a Dominican Army colonel who went by the single name of "Bayonet," sent along a small squad of soldiers to accompany us.

The lush Dominican landscape had the feel of a tropical paradise, but the poverty I witnessed on the drive toward the heliport appeared staggering. Once on board, we flew past the southern coastal town of San Pedro de Macoris, famous for being the home turf of so many major league shortstops, and headed north toward San Francisco de Macoris. Through the open door next to me I heard the roar of the rotors and caught the heavy scent of foliage from the dense forest below. I had to steel myself against holding on for dear life.

The helicopter took us over a stretch of ocean that Tom Cash pointed out as a major drop-off point where the planes and ships bringing drugs into Santo Domingo transferred their loads. The cargo was later smuggled into Florida and other points in the U.S.

The pilot hovered for a time over a luxury resort on the northern coast, near Puerto Plata. I wondered why we were lingering so long, until I saw the Dominican soldiers scrambling over each other to get a view down onto the grounds of the hotel. The place catered to European tourists and the female guests sunbathed topless in the Continental manner. So as well as a law enforcement fact-finding tour, the trip was also a sightseeing occasion for the army guys.

The Blackhawk pilot swooped along the northeast coast and I caught sight of an area of large, mansion-like homes, their roofs dotted with multiple satellite dishes. The landscaped grounds of every estate featured gorgeous swimming pools, and the long driveways were lined with beautiful cars—Mercedes, BMW sedans, and luxury SUVs.

"Drug palaces," Cash shouted out to me over the sound of the helicopter, gesturing to the enormous haciendas below. The satellite dishes, I understood, indicated the wealth accumulated by the owners. They needed state-of-the-art communications to control their smuggling empires.

The difference between the luxury of the estates and the squalid poverty of the Santo Domingo back alleys could not have been more extreme. The contrast disheartened me. It symbolized the brutal dynamic that lured so many people into drug trafficking, those who believed that the only exit from the slums was a life in the violent world of narcotics.

In 1995 I was interviewed by CBS's Morley Safer for a *60*

Minutes report about the Dominican drug trade. Safer told the story of two mothers whose sons went to America to make money dealing narcotics. One son came back to the D.R. in a body bag, while the other returned with enough money to build a palace such as I saw on my fact-finding visit. Success or death seemed to be the only options for so many of the island's promising young people.

I had a theoretical knowledge of drug networks, but that Blackhawk trip made the situation crystal clear, and something clicked into place. I knew the troubled neighborhood of Washington Heights back home in New York City, where many of the residents came from backgrounds in the Dominican Republic. The bustling streets of Washington Heights and the expensive coastal estates I saw below me were separated by fifteen hundred miles, but intimately connected through vast webs of money, violence, and drugs.

We've got our work cut out for us, I thought to myself.

The job of working with the DEA and going after the major drug organizations belonged to the Special Investigations Bureau (SIB), created by Sterling Johnson years before I came to Special Narcotics. It targeted criminal drug organizations of national or international scope, oftentimes tracing back to the source of the flow of product coming into New York City. Allied closely with the DEA and the NYPD, the bureau prosecuted major cases.

A few blocks away from the SNP's headquarters at 80 Centre, SIB maintained its own separate office. This arrangement made it possible for informants—of which Special Investigations had many—to arrive secretly. The SIB was comprised of terrifically smart, dedicated, and indefatigable individuals who all had something of the bulldog in them. Chief among them was the woman who would eventually step into my position as head of Special Narcotics, who is still in this position today.

Bridget Brennan had a deeply felt instinct for the rule of law. She came to the office in 1983 and served in various high-profile roles, including Director of Training. She once briefly acted as the Boss's press secretary.

I lured Bridget over to Special Narcotics in January 1992, naming her as the Deputy Chief of the Special Investigations Bureau. Megan Dodd was then the Chief of SIB, and when she went out on maternity leave and decided to come back as Counsel to SIB, Bridget became the head of Special Investigations. She did a superb job in both managing the cases and running the bureau. She got up to speed quickly on the pending investigations, developed a good rapport with DEA agents, and was respected by the SIB assistants.

We were making big cases and doing great things. It's ironic, but before I came to Special Narcotics, the road ran only one way: people left Special Narcotics because they wanted to get back "across the street" to the courtrooms of 100 Centre, where they believed the real action was. I now had ADAs pleading to come the other way, from 100 Centre to Special Narcotics, many of them wanting to join the Special Investigations Bureau.

When publisher, philanthropist, and former United States Ambassador to Britain Walter H. Annenberg contributed his art collection to New York City's Metropolitan Museum, I recall that he explained his gift by commenting, "strength goes to strength." He meant that the Met's holdings were so strong that his own extensive collection would find a good home there.

"Strength goes to strength" is a principle and a dynamic that applies to many areas of human endeavor. Because Special Narcotics was demonstrating such prowess in the prosecutorial field, I was able to recruit some very strong assistants to cross over to SIB, which made the office all the more effective.

The Special Investigations Bureau and Special Narcotics helped prosecute a series of memorable cases:

- A sprawling investigation headed up by ADA Mari Maloney came to be known as the "Apple Pie Gang" because of details we learned from wiretaps. The Cali cartel installed an operative nicknamed Caliche in a suburban Long Island home they were using as a base of operations. The Colombians were smart. They had a strict policy of keeping money and drugs in separate locations, so that they could limit their losses in cases of discovery. Our wiretap monitors listened in as one of the bosses instructed Caliche on the nuances of American middle-class life. It's important to blend in, the boss said. "Act as an American family," he instructed. "Eat apple pie. Always buy a *TV Guide*, because that's the American bible. Take your garbage out, stay away from the house during working hours, nine-to-five, just like a good husband would who has a job. Even though you don't speak English, subscribe to newspapers like everyone else on the block." The subterfuge didn't help. In May 1993 the house was busted anyhow, one of a series of seven coordinated raids. Agents arrested Caliche and four other dealers, seizing $10 million in cash and over four tons of cocaine all told, nationwide. The repercussions spread throughout the country, as twenty-five Cali cartel operatives were arrested and charged with drug trafficking offenses.

- The epic tale of *Phoenix*, a sixty-five foot, twin mast, steel hulled sailboat specially equipped for smuggling, began in the wiretap rooms of the DEA Task Force.

Around the same time as the Caliche bust, Eddie Beach and his team of DEA Task Force agents picked up the trail of *Phoenix* in Ecuador, installed a tracking device in the mast, and followed it to docking at a port in Galveston, Texas. As in the cans-of-tomatoes case, agents had a difficult time locating the drug stash on the boat, spending almost a full day searching before they found a secret compartment beneath a sheath of concrete in the keel. Haul: fifteen hundred kilos of cocaine, over one-and-a-half tons.

• Cocaine and Carrots: In March 1997 the DEA seized a tractor trailer with Texas license plates in Corona, Queens. The trailer was packed to the roof with 60,000 pounds of carrots—and, hidden among the four-by-four-foot bins of vegetables, two tons of cocaine. The enormous stash was headed for the streets of Washington Heights and would have generated millions in retail sales. The seizure was the largest in New York history, the result of a seven-month investigation by SIB and the DEA Task force, leading to nine arrests, including ringleader Geraldo Gonzalez. Another $1.3 million in cash was taken from one of Gonzalez's apartments, a safe house that didn't turn out to be all that safe.

These types of cases engendered a great deal of press attention. You may recall press conferences and newspaper articles where all the representatives of the various law enforcement agencies involved spoke, and all the drugs, guns, and money seized were on display on a table in front of them.

As Special Narcotics Prosecutor, I made sure to come prepared so I felt quite comfortable speaking at these press conferences. I realized early on how the process worked: the Mayor or the Police

Commissioner would speak, followed by me and officials from the other agencies involved. I would get my own thirty seconds—and literally, that's usually all that would be given to me.

"I am pleased that we were able to take several leaders of a violent drug gang off the streets," I said in one instance. "They call themselves the Bloods, and we closed off an artery."

A sense of humor made for good copy, even if it was pretty dark humor, given the circumstances. But I always tried to come up with a succinct and memorable line. I understood that the reporters needed a quotable soundbite. They didn't even particularly care what the content of the quote might be. What they wanted was something quick and easy.

Despite being lauded by the press, Special Narcotics had other ways to celebrate our successes. I made sure to hold separate, non-media events whenever we broke a big case. I would bring in the DEA or NYPD unit that made the case and commemorate the event with a group photo. The idea was to give credit where credit was due, making all those involved know that they were a part of the operation, that it would not have succeeded without them.

"A lot of people are real eager to *take* credit," DEA's Carlo Boccia once said to the press. "But Bob is one of those people who goes out of his way to *give* credit."

It seemed to me like a principle of Management 101. I thought the folks in the trenches, those working the surveillance, for example, deserved a tremendous amount of credit. They might not appear at a press conference, but I wanted to make sure they were recognized.

CHAPTER 19

END OF AN ERA

D uring the mid-1990s, I experienced a sense of conflicted emotions. Most strongly, I felt proud of all that we had accomplished during my tenure at Special Narcotics. I could look back with no apologies and a sense of having made a real difference. However, I also started to have thoughts of whether it was time for me to move on.

I recall meeting with Howard Safir one day over lunch. He had just taken over the post of New York City Police Commissioner from Bill Bratton, so it must have been some time in 1996. Safir had a distinguished career in law enforcement and had served as Giuliani's Fire Commissioner before being named Police Commissioner.

"I feel the city is changing," I told Safir. "The crime numbers are down. People are returning to the city. They're going back to Times Square to see shows."

Safir agreed. He said, "the crime situation has improved dramatically and the City is headed in the right direction." We were like a pair of ship's captains, with vessels that had at least partially righted themselves after a storm.

"You know, Howard," I went on, "I think the thing I'm most proud of, what has really changed the city, was the dismantling of the violent drug gangs. I remember when every other day you would hear about drive-by shootings. Now you don't hear about it anymore. They're no longer happening."

This success of targeting drug trafficking organizations hadn't been accomplished overnight. It took hard work, and the concerted efforts of the NYPD, the assistant district attorneys on my staff, the DEA Task Force, other law enforcement agencies, and committed, energetic judges such as Leslie Crocker Snyder.

I told Safir, "The people who are really getting the benefit of all this are the tens of thousands who are living in the city housing projects, which were just inundated by these drug gangs. There'd be shootings there every day and there'd be robberies. People were afraid to leave their houses, afraid for their kids to walk the streets and go to school. Now all that's different, and that's a dramatic change. We really did better the lives of all these people by taking out these drug gangs."

"I agree," Safir said. "There's a direct, traceable relationship between the work you did at SNP and the change in the city that you're talking about."

Oddly enough, that sense of accomplishment allowed me to think about the unthinkable. I didn't speak about it to Safir, but I was already considering leaving public service for the private sector.

I felt pinched by a pair of concerns. One was an awareness that, for all we had accomplished, I had taken the position of Special Narcotics Prosecutor about as far as it could go. I found myself feeling stale, as though I had run out of fresh ideas. I was tired of the late night calls, and those occasions that necessitated police cars guarding my home and family.

My second concern was that I needed money. The necessity of paying college tuition for my children loomed before me. After more than two decades as a public servant, I was rich in experience but relatively impoverished in my bank account.

At first it felt impossible, the idea of saying good-bye to the place where I had built my entire professional career. I took a temperature reading among my friends and colleagues. More than one told me the same thing: the time to leave is when you're on top. During my final year in the office, we had made a number of major drug busts. I personally had gotten my share of publicity, including a laudatory profile in *Newsday* and one in the *New York Daily News*, where the headline referred to me glowingly: "Secret Weapon Vs. Crime."

When I announced I was leaving SNP and DANY in 1997— making sure I informed the Boss first, so that Morgenthau would not feel blindsided—I had an incredible valedictory sense of an era ending.

I knew that I was leaving Special Narcotics in extremely capable hands. Bridget Brennan would take over the leadership and usher it into an age of designer drugs, legal opioids, and encrypted digital communications—thorny problems that I was actually pretty thankful not to have to face.

On May 1, 1998, the city's five District Attorneys appointed Bridget Brennan as Special Narcotics Prosecutor. I knew she would be terrific, and that proved to be the case. I witnessed her progress from afar, while under her direction the office developed innovative strategies to target emerging problems.

I experienced a long goodbye. I had a great deal of affection for all those who worked with me along the way, from my days as a Trial Preparation Assistant up to my time at Special Narcotics, and every stop in between.

I had a number of going-away parties. The first occurred on November 7, 1997, at the SPQR restaurant in Little Italy, where I was the DANY Association guest of honor. Another larger get-together came almost a month later, at the Downtown Athletic Club on December 2, 1997.

The venue was the longtime site of glamorous dinners announcing the Heisman Trophy winners. The annual award for the nation's outstanding college football player was named for John Heisman, the club's first athletic director. I felt aware of the irony of me, a Bronx kid with childhood dreams of becoming a sports star, winding up being feted for a very different brand of achievement in a space where athletic heroes had claimed their trophies.

The banquet was sold out. Not only that, but there was a waiting list to get tickets. The evening was hosted by Peter Kougasian. DEA chief Tom Constantine flew in from Washington. Other luminaries came in from around the country. The evening started with a procession of the NYPD bagpipers presenting the colors, a tremendous honor.

Morgenthau sat next to me that night. He looked around at the gathering and said, "I've never seen so many different agencies represented at a going away dinner."

I picked out many faces in the crowd that I warmly recognized, people who I had worked alongside in cases large and small. They were my colleagues and, in many instances, my friends. I was overwhelmed by conflicting emotions—love and happiness for the gratitude expressed by those I knew and admired, sadness at the idea of leaving the professional environment where I had become acquainted with so many remarkable individuals.

When it came time for my remarks, I tried to lighten my emotional mood with humor. "I entered DANY looking like Robert Redford," I said. "Today I take leave of it looking like Danny DeVito."

I must have received over twenty awards that night, recognition extended by the FBI, the DEA (as well as the DEA Task Force), the New York State Police, the New York City Police Department, the Secret Service, the Bureau of Alcohol, Tobacco and Firearms, and U.S. Customs. Both the U.S. Attorneys from the Eastern and Southern Districts sent citations of service. The office of New

York State Governor George Pataki provided a letter of recognition.

Morgenthau would formally respond to my resignation letter with a letter of his own, the last paragraph of which I treasure:

> "The high regard in which you are held by all of our associates testifies to your outstanding qualities of character and personality. Your many friends and former colleagues join me in extending our best wishes to you . . . and that you will enjoy continued success, good health and happiness."

Thanks, Boss.

I never had much personal interaction with Mayor Guiliani. I found him to be very smart, with a huge ego. He surrounded himself with a bright and loyal group of advisors, many of whom worked with him when he was the United States Attorney for the Southern District of New York. People I knew in the administration told me that he was a tireless worker, but was very vindictive. He would make it a point to go after his critics and enemies.

Shortly before I left Special Narcotics, Guiliani had one of his citywide meetings at New York Law School. There was a large crowd in attendance, including brass from the police and fire departments, the district attorneys' offices, correction, probation, budget and other agencies. When I arrived at the meeting I was told by Colleen Roche, Guiliani's Press Secretary, to sit in the front row. Colleen, who I knew when she used to work at DANY, must have told Guiliani that I was leaving public service. Much to my surprise, when the meeting was ending, Rudy asked me to stand and informed the crowd that he wanted to thank me for all that I accomplished during my career, and for helping to make New York a safer city. I received a standing ovation and was truly honored that the mayor would do that for me. After the meeting he invited me over to take pictures with him at City Hall. Guiliani is a big Yankee fan, so we had an enjoyable fifteen-minute discussion about the team. It was a truly memorable experience.

Of course, I had thoroughly thought over my options upon leaving SNP. The office of Special Narcotics Prosecutor was about as high as I could climb in my professional field in New York City—unless I wanted to run for elective office, a prospect for which I had no appetite at all. The brief flirtation I had with the idea of campaigning for Nassau County District Attorney—"the best decision I never made"—cured me of that.

There was always Washington, D.C., a little over two hundred miles to the south of New York City, but in another sense light years away.

Over the years I experienced a few opportunities to deal with Congress or the U.S. Department of Justice. During the Clinton years, for example, elements within Justice floated the idea of merging the Drug Enforcement Administration with the Federal Bureau of Investigation, creating some kind of DEA/FBI hybrid superagency. I had worked with agents of both entities and thought it was a terrible idea. At the invitation of Charles Schumer, then not yet a senator but a representative in the House, I journeyed down to the capital to testify before a congressional committee.

"With drug trafficking offenses," I told the committee members, "we're not talking about a robbery case or a murder case, but about very fluid organizations that move illicit substances internationally. The FBI is a generalist organization. The agents there deal with a number of different aspects of crime. But the

DEA specializes in one thing, and that's drug trafficking. The DEA personnel I've worked with know their field better than anyone on the planet. To merge these tremendously committed agents into another organization makes little sense."

While I was in Washington, I went to see Janet Reno, who was then U.S. Attorney General. At that time, she was seeking to fill the post of DEA Administrator. The outgoing administrator was a former federal judge named Robert C. Bonner. There were two candidates in the mix, former New York City Police Commissioner Raymond Kelly and Thomas Constantine, who was the head of the New York State Police. I always had solid relationships with both men, working with them often while at Special Narcotics.

"Between the two of them, Kelly and Constantine," Reno asked me, "what do you think?"

I knew the old rule of thumb that discretion is the better part of valor, and I gave Reno a careful, political answer. "Madam Attorney General, I don't think you could go wrong selecting either one of them. They're both excellent choices."

"Do you have any interest in the job?" she asked.

"I'll just answer that by saying once again you couldn't go wrong with either Kelly or Constantine."

Reno laughed and nodded. I believe Reno's suggestion was a pro forma compliment rather than a serious offer. I don't think I ever would have been chosen anyway. A short time later Tom Constantine was selected for the position.

Later on, I performed another brief *pas de deux* with Washington when my name was mentioned for the position of Drug Czar. From experience I knew this was a no-win proposition. "Drug Czar" was a title for what was essentially a do-nothing job. It was an inside-the-beltway, policy-wonk position, officially titled the Director of the Office of National Drug Control Policy.

I shuddered at the idea of myself in Washington, churning out white papers and reports, trudging from one committee hearing to another.

So going to D.C. wasn't really an option. I was too far along in my career to enter the rugby scrum of national politics. It would mean a daily slog of back-and-forth DC-NYC trips, either on Acela or the airline shuttle. I knew people who had done that routine, and it wasn't a great lifestyle. The alternative choice would be to uproot Shelley and my family from our happy home in New York.

No thank you.

The private sphere beckoned.

CHAPTER 20

LIFE AFTER SNP

My eventual departure from SNP came via a contact I made through an organization called the Federal Drug Agents Foundation. The good work these folks do centers on providing support to families of DEA agents downed in action or otherwise in need of help—a child of an officer who requires surgery, for example. Eventually, the foundation's work expanded to provide aid to any police officer or law enforcement agency.

The organization was made up primarily of business people. Dennis Schnur served as the longtime chairman of the board, whom I knew because of my history working with the Drug Enforcement Administration. One of the people involved in the foundation was a lawyer by the name of Gary Katz. On one occasion, Dennis Schnur took the directors of the charity foundation over to Special Narcotics to have me talk about current aspects of the drug problem and give them a tour of the office. On that occasion, I had a conversation with Katz.

"I represent a man named Mark Nathanson," he said. The name meant nothing to me, but it soon would. He was a Canadian who had started up a company called Forensic Investigative Associates—FIA for short.

"Nathanson has offices in Canada, the U.K., Cyprus, and Moscow," Katz told me. "He wants to open a branch of FIA in the States."

At Katz's behest, I agreed to take a get-to-know-you call with

Rod Stamler, who had retired as one of the leading figures in the Royal Canadian Mounted Police. Stamler headed up FIA. After the call, I did a little due diligence looking into my prospective future employer. It's always good to know who you might be getting into bed with.

What I discovered fascinated me. As a boy, Mark Nathanson had always wanted to be a cop. But he couldn't afford to live on a cop's wages, so he became a businessman instead. In the 1980s, he found himself in the mining trade, poring over maps of West Africa, prospecting for big finds. After a period of intense analysis, he was able to say "dig here" to his financial backers.

His instincts—and his research—proved true. In Mali, his company struck the biggest gold deposit in the country's history, a vein containing some eight million ounces of the precious metal.

"I felt like I had discovered King Solomon's mine," Nathanson told me later.

He started a company on the Canadian stock exchange in Toronto called International African Mining Gold Company, listed by the eye-catching name of IAMGOLD. Investors flocked to the new prospect.

When the real money started pouring in, Nathanson had the resources to do whatever he wanted, and decided he would follow his childhood dream of law enforcement. An added motivation was that he'd experienced plenty of corrupt practices in governments around the world, and he wanted to find ways to combat such graft.

He donated four million dollars to York University's Osgoode Law School in Toronto to endow the Jack and Mae Nathanson Centre for Transnational Human Rights, Crime and Security, named after his parents and funding research on crime and corruption.

He also tailored FIA to be, among other things, an anti-corruption watchdog. Through his international connections he opened an FIA office in Cyprus, because he knew the former head of intelligence and former chief of police there. Via another connection, he brought in a former KGB agent and opened an FIA office in Moscow, then an office in London headed by a former higher-up in Scotland Yard.

But FIA as of yet had no presence anywhere in the U.S.

"We're looking to open up an office in the United States," Katz told me. "We need someone to head it. Would you be interested in that?"

Intrigued by the whole Nathanson story, and with one eye on my children's college tuition payments coming up, I expressed an interest in taking an exploratory next step. Nathanson flew me to Canada, and the two of us hit it off immediately.

The mining mogul was an eccentric guy, but at the same time down-to-earth, accessible, and friendly. "I'd love for you to run the U.S. operation of the company," he said.

"You know, Mark, I have a family to support," I told him. "Right now I have a job that I can keep forever, until I retire, so it'll take something special for me to make the leap."

In the consulting and investigations field, there's little job security, and an employee can be hired and fired at will. Having been in government all my life, my other concern was that I didn't really know anything about running a business. I was leery of not being able to make a go of it.

"It may take some time to make this company successful," I said.

"Well, what are you looking for?" Nathanson asked.

"A three-year contract," I answered. If I was going to jump, I needed a secure place to land.

"I understand that," Nathanson said. "I'll tell you what we'll do. I want to make sure that you have no worries about money, as well as have an incentive to build up this company. So I'll pay you your entire three-year salary upfront."

Such extravagant measures are why we label figures like Nathanson "Lords of the Universe." Great, right? But not so fast, I thought.

"That's very enticing," I said. "I'm not an accountant, but for tax purposes a lump sum is probably not the best thing."

"All right," he said. "I'll put your entire three-year salary in escrow, to be paid to you every two weeks, so you don't have to worry about it."

It was a deal too good to refuse. We agreed on a salary, a signing bonus, and part ownership of the U.S. company.

That was the summer of 1997. My last day at Special Narcotics was November 7, and I started at the newly created New York FIA office the following Monday, November 10. In fitting with the international nature of the firm, we located ourselves near the United Nations, at 3rd Avenue near East 48th Street. I had to take a test to get my P.I., my private investigator's license, which I passed. We were now ready to open the doors of FIA, USA.

Around this time, I returned to SNP to have lunch with Bridget Brennan. Everyone was glad to see me and I got hugs all around. But the experience sobered me. *I don't belong here anymore*, I remember thinking. That visit was the turning point, the realization that my tenure had irrevocably ended. Physically, I was already out the door. But now I was emotionally able to move on to the private sector.

In my new position, business began to take off right from the start. Apart from a secretary, my first hire was a former U.S. Customs agent to work on investigations. I also needed a really solid second-in-command. I called my good friend, Steve Gutstein, who had worked with me in the DA's office, and whom I had known and trusted for many years. Steve was very bright, a terrific writer with excellent judgment. He was someone I could count on, someone I could run things by, who would give me true and unsparing feedback. He was certainly not a yes man. He had gone into private practice and I lured him to FIA—to come in out of the cold, so to speak.

As the company grew, we started bringing in more and more researchers. The consulting and investigations business always reminded me of the original TV version of *Mission Impossible*, about a team of espionage agents. I recalled the disembodied voice on the tape recorder, talking to team leader Jim Phelps, played by actor Peter Graves. "Your mission, Jim, should you decide to accept it . . ." Phelps would get the undercover assignment, and then he would open his folder containing photos of his operatives. Assembling his team, he would take out this or that picture—an explosives expert, a master of disguise, etc. In my case, I would listen to a client seeking FIA's help.

"You tell me what the problem is," I would say, channeling *Mission Impossible*. "Once I understand what the problem is, I'll assemble the team to deal with that problem."

We developed a great working relationship with a prestigious investment firm, which became one of our best clients. The firm would often want FIA to research companies that they considered doing multi-million-dollar international financial deals with. Soon word of the quality of our work spread throughout the investment community, and we brought in more and more business from the financial sphere.

I was often asked by clients, "Is there any place in the world where you could not get information?"

I thought about it. Antarctica, maybe? But on second thought, didn't we have among our contacts at FIA a Russian security guy who formerly worked at Vostok Station, a research institute in the Antarctic? I remembered a case we did in Andorra, a small country in the Pyrenees mountains, between France and Spain, that not many people could find on a map. The globe has a lot of nooks and crannies, but FIA had a wide range of techniques for sniffing them out. I don't think there was anywhere we couldn't develop intel on.

Throughout my years at the DA's office, and especially at Special Narcotics, I had developed many international contacts. Quite a few DEA agents who had been posted abroad grew to like the life in their host countries and wound up retiring overseas. For example, the agent who once ran the DEA office in the Philippines retired, married a woman he had met on the job, and settled there. The same thing happened in Singapore.

All I had to do was reach out to my network. I was able to secure tremendously valuable information on a variety of overseas matters.

FIA had an assignment once in Denmark. I contacted someone I knew who was the head of the DEA office in Scandinavia. He introduced me to a gentleman who lived in Denmark who was a retired cop. He was able to get me all the information I needed in Denmark. Later on, when I had a problem in Sweden, I called on the retired cop in Denmark. It turned out he had a friend who was a former cop in Sweden.

And that's how things get done.

The New York office of the firm brought in a tremendous amount of business. Mark Nathanson was thrilled because he loved the ins and outs and the whole aura of law enforcement. He was a "police buff" in every sense of the word. I got him involved with several police organizations, and he became a member of the Federal Drug Agents Foundation. FIA's founder and godfather was happy as could be.

Beyond our investigations work, we also developed an area of expertise in monitoring businesses and other entities that had found themselves in trouble and under court-ordered limitations.

As Mayor of New York City, Rudy Giuliani embarked on a campaign to crack down on unruly nightclubs. Busted for noise abatement and the sale of drugs at their venues, by agreement the clubs could only reopen if they followed strict guidelines. The NYPD came to me at FIA and asked the company to function as a monitor, ensuring the clubs were toeing the line.

I had a history at Special Narcotics with Peter Gatien, the nightlife impresario. The city was concerned with drug use at the Limelight, one of his clubs, an infamous hot spot located in a former church on Sixth Avenue, in New York City's Chelsea neighborhood. Authorities had shuttered the place more than once, including in 1995, when Special Narcotics worked with the NYPD to close it down.

A few years later, an attorney from the law firm that represented Gatien contacted me. The Tunnel, another Gatien club on the far West Side of Manhattan, had been closed, unable to reopen without a plan for abiding with nuisance abatement laws and the use and sale of narcotics in the club. "Peter Gatien needs someone to be a monitor for compliance," the lawyer said. "Someone who can advise Gatien on how to keep drugs from being used or sold in his clubs."

I couldn't believe what I was hearing. "I think you've wasted your time," I told him. "You want Peter Gatien to hire me as a monitor? He'll never go for it. I was the one who shut his Limelight nightclub down!"

"You don't understand," the lawyer said. "Peter Gatien actually requested you personally. He said you were a straight shooter who had treated him fairly."

Peter realized that if I could close his clubs down, then I could figure out how to keep them open. In that way, my former target became a client. We became friends and had a good working relationship.

With the Tunnel on board at FIA, other nightclubs under review by Giuliani and the NYPD hired the company as a monitor. Without really trying to, I suddenly found myself the new "King of Clubs" in New York City. No squarer man for the job could they have found. But I knew how to monitor for compliance.

Oddly enough, for a sector that I had essentially backed into, monitoring became one of the best bread-and-butter businesses at FIA. We were so well known for expertise in that area we began to get calls from all over the country. A huge club in Panama City, Florida, which had been featured by MTV on the channel's spring break coverage, came to us. The club had problems with a court in Florida, and with the local prosecutor's office. The owners took us on as monitors.

FIA's reach had become nationwide. Business boomed. Within a few years of its founding, the U.S. branch of FIA was flourishing. But even though we were outdoing all of the other FIA offices, personal considerations intruded on our success. Nathanson's wife became ill and he lost interest in the company.

Robert Tucker, a former Special Assistant to the Queens DA Richard Brown and grandson of renowned operatic tenor Richard Tucker, owned a security guard firm called T&M Protection Resources. He was looking to expand. Tucker hired Joe Russo, head of former President Bill Clinton's Secret Service detail, to start up an Executive Protection Division.

Tucker also wanted to get into the world of investigations. In 2004, he bought FIA from Nathanson. Tucker basically wanted just me and the U.S. operation and jettisoned all the other international offices. Creating an investigation division within T&M, Tucker decided to keep the FIA name because of its success and the value of its name recognition. FIA officially merged into the larger company in 2013, when I decided to step down as President of FIA. I then became the Special Advisor to the CEO, a position I still hold to the present day.

After the T&M acquisition of FIA, the new Investigative Division continued to thrive. Monitorships became the company's cash cow. We continued to monitor nightclubs, but we also branched out to real estate companies, construction companies, and carting companies (aka trash-hauling businesses, a field that historically was deeply mobbed up).

The work was varied and spread across several different fields of endeavor. When prisoners brought a successful class action lawsuit for being improperly searched, the federal judge in the case appointed FIA as a Special Master to monitor compliance. The United States Attorney's Office for the Southern District selected FIA to monitor a healthcare agency. I even got an assignment to prepare an investigative manual for New York City's Department of Correction.

Our biggest success occurred when FIA was brought in to set up a nationwide secret-shopper program to monitor the retail practices of a financial services firm that was accused of predatory lending practices. The engagement lasted for over five years and brought over thirty million dollars of revenue into FIA's coffers.

The more I worked with people and companies under the gun from the legal system, the more I came to better understand the defense side than I did when I worked as a prosecutor. I was reminded that there are two sides to every story, and that not every case is black and white.

Generally, when I was at FIA and later at T&M, I pretty much avoided any dealings with the Manhattan DA's office, and especially SNP. I just felt uncomfortable about being on the other side and dealing with my old friends and colleagues. A few times I dealt with DANY when I was brought on as a monitor and had to turn in a report or meet with a staffer at the office regarding the monitorship.

So it was unusual when Mike Mansfield, a former chief in the Queens DA's office and city commissioner who had joined T&M, told me there was a client he wanted to help that had a case with DANY.

"I've been brought into a case that involves an owner of a lot of Irish bars in Manhattan," Mansfield said. If you know New York City at all, you know "Blarney Stone"-style Irish pubs are a fixture of the urban landscape. A collection of such bars represented the whole of the client's business.

"He had a friend who was a building inspector," Mansfield went on. "What happened was, he paid some money to the building inspector. What the building inspector would always do for him was basically expedite things like inspections and certificates of occupancy."

Another thing is clear if you know New York City at all, which is that the bureaucracy can be agonizingly slow and fiendishly complex. From building permits to liquor licenses, getting a response from a city office can be a frustrating process.

As part of a citywide law enforcement sting targeting corrupt city officials, the client was caught on tape giving money to his inspector pal.

By his lawyer's account, the pub owner was a good guy with no arrest record. He owned several establishments that were close to the Twin Towers during the 9/11 attacks, and he had donated huge amounts of food and drink to the workers during the downtown Manhattan recovery effort. Meanwhile, the DA's office was playing hardball, offering him a plea bargain that retained the felony bribery charge brought against him.

A felony conviction meant the pub owner could kiss his multiple liquor licenses goodbye. It was essentially a death sentence for his businesses.

"Take a look at this," Mansfield said. He showed me a batch of forty-one letters that were written in support of the pub owner, glowing character references that testified what a credit he was to the community. After reading the letters, I determined that it would be an injustice for this man to have to plead guilty to a felony and as a result lose his liquor license and his businesses. I told Mansfield that I would reach out to the DA's office and see what I could do.

I made an appointment to see Jodie Kane, Chief of the Rackets Bureau at DANY, which is where the pub owner's case was being prosecuted. Though I never worked directly with Kane when I was in the DA's office, I knew her and the excellent reputation she had earned.

"I never get involved with active cases," I said to her. "But this would be a real miscarriage of justice. For a guy like this, who's sixty-two years old, has no criminal record, and dealt generously with the 9/11 first responders, a felony charge would be a shame. What did he do? He gave money to a guy he knew from his childhood in Ireland to get a Certificate of Occupancy more quickly."

Eventually, the case went all the way up to Cyrus Vance, who had succeeded Morgenthau as the Manhattan District Attorney. In the name of fairness, Vance allowed the pub owner to plead guilty to a misdemeanor.

Justice done.

There's a kicker to the story. In 2015, when Pope Francis

held mass at Manhattan's Central Park, the Federal Drug Agents Foundation received a request from the Secret Service. The security detail for the Pope needed to set up a command post in downtown Manhattan. Did the Foundation know of anyone who could donate food and drink for the agents?

I asked Mansfield to call the attorney for the pub owner and ask if he would step up. He always said he couldn't thank us enough for what we did for him. Mansfield didn't have to beg. The pub owner donated $6,000 toward food and drinks for the Secret Service command post. A nice gesture, and a willing one for an Irish Catholic to make in service of the Pope.

Oh, I know what kind of cynical comment could be made about this whole incident. One hand washes the other, you know? I helped this guy keep his license and yes, he felt indebted and supplied the command post. But tit-for-tat reciprocal arrangements were never a big part of my professional life. I made an exception in this case, in the name of justice and fair play.

Sometimes, what happens when one hand washes the other is that both parties wind up a little cleaner than they were before.

CHAPTER 21

A LOOK BACK AT MY LIFE

P icture me these days with my wife, Shelley, watching *The Undoing*, a streaming TV series starring Nicole Kidman and Hugh Grant. In the middle of an episode comes a shot of 100 Centre's expansive front entrance. The scene features a crowd of reporters and TV cameras confronting the Hugh Grant character, Dr. Jonathan Fraser. I feel a flood of nostalgia.

"I've been in those courtrooms so many times," I say wistfully. But I also experience annoyance over the obvious departures from reality that constantly crop up. Whenever we watch a show based on the criminal justice system, I keep a running commentary of the flaws that I notice.

"That kind of thing never happens," I mutter as an aside to Shelley. She is used to me critiquing the fabrications of Hollywood when treating material that I know so well. It's just one more measure of how public perception rarely gets the legal system exactly right, which is another reason I wrote this book. I wanted to give people a real look at what actually happens in the criminal justice system.

When I reflect on my life and career, I shake my head and laugh about how a street kid from the Bronx with little family money and no connections made it all the way to the top and literally became the nation's top drug prosecutor. I think about how lucky and blessed I am. I also think about how fortuitous life is and how the decisions we make or don't make affect our lives.

Suppose I decided not to go the beach with a friend that day, or say it rained. I would not have met Shelley. Suppose my law school friend never mentioned that DANY was looking to hire trial preparation assistants or I never followed up on it. Where would I have ended up practicing law? Where would my career have ended up if I turned down Morgenthau's request that I go to Special Narcotics? Sometimes we make the right life decisions and sometimes we don't. Sometimes we take chances and they turn out okay, other times they don't. Sometimes I think of the Lewis Carroll line, "In the end . . . We only regret the chances we didn't take." I have been lucky for the most part. I made the right decisions and took the right chances. I have always tried to use good judgment and common sense when weighing the pros and cons before making important decisions. I also worked hard, including teaching full time while going to law school four nights a week for four years.

I remember reading the Jim Collins bestseller, *Good to Great*, about why some good companies turn into great companies and others fail. When the CEO's of the great companies were interviewed, they all mentioned that they were lucky, that luck played a role in their success. Collins surmised that they put themselves in a position to be lucky by making the right decisions, or by bringing in the right people to help them.

I was "lucky" in that I was given opportunities and handled them successfully. I still wonder why Morgenthau selected an inexperienced third year ADA to form and lead the new Juvenile Offense Bureau. However, given the opportunity, I was successful in prosecuting two page one murder cases, which led to the change in juvenile laws not only in New York, but other states as well. It was that success that gave Morgenthau the confidence to promote me to a deputy bureau chief's position, and later to a bureau chief's position. My success in those positions and ability to deal with people led Morgenthau to choose me to go Special Narcotics, which I fortunately accepted. When given the opportunity to become the Special Narcotics Prosecutor, I was smart enough to surround myself with a top-flight managerial staff. I was also lucky enough to work with some great police officers and federal agents and make important connections throughout the world, which turned out to be very helpful once I entered the private sector.

Upon deciding to leave Special Narcotics, I was lucky enough to be introduced to Gary Katz, the attorney for Mark Nathanson, who spoke with me about the opportunity to run the United States operations of Forensic Investigative Associates. I had no experience or knowledge of how to run a business in the private sector, since I had no clients and had been a government employee my whole professional life. Fortunately, I was able to pick things up quickly and successfully handle the work that came in. I was able to grow the business thanks in part to many of my former loyal assistants and contacts that sent me business. With their help and my success in dealing with clients, FIA and later T& M flourished.

Today, thanks to my luck and success, I am able to enjoy life, my wife, my children and their spouses, and especially my five wonderful grandchildren.

I guess in the end I was lucky and good at what I did. If I can give myself a pat on the back, sometimes good guys do finish first.

A FINAL WORD

Today when I open a newspaper or turn on the evening news at home, I often feel a sense of dread. Of course, in these uncertain times there is a lot to be dismayed about. But my reaction is triggered by more specific concerns, based on my experience. The previous pages of this book detailed issues that I dealt with during my professional career: the widespread use of illicit drugs, the episodes of extreme juvenile violence, and the violent crime that New York City and the country experienced in the seventies, eighties, and early nineties.

Unfortunately, I currently see society slipping back to those bad old days.

In 1990, the city's annual murder rate had spiraled upward, hitting a peak of 2,605. People now in their forties or younger have no recollection of how entire neighborhoods of New York City were "no-go" areas after dark, how drive-by shootings were a regular occurrence, and how graffiti marked every building and subway car. Times Square was not a friendly tourist stop, but a zone rife with muggers, prostitutes, and petty thieves instead of colorful, costumed characters. Pickpockets and scam artists fed off the Broadway theater crowds as a basis for the local street economy.

Then, as the situation started to change in the mid-nineties, the rate of violent crime fell. Society seemed to right itself somewhat. New York City became a more livable place. Times Square saw an influx of new visitors as family-oriented attractions replaced sex shows.

But, after a two-decade dip in major crime of historic pro-portions, the pendulum has started to swing the other way. The country recently just recorded the biggest spike in the murder rate in six decades, along with a terrifying resurgence in street violence. Chicago's 797 homicides in 2021 represent the highest number in a quarter century, and the most of any U.S. city. Drug overdose deaths in the nation routinely top 100,000 per year, and opioids kill an average of 136 Americans per day.

The rate of homicides committed by juvenile offenders had once fallen from its peak, which occurred during the Bosket-Olave era that I experienced firsthand. But judging by current anecdotal accounts, the problem still exists.

I read of the recent armed carjacking of a U.S. Congresswoman by five teenagers in South Philadelphia, including a fourteen-year-old girl, and three males ages thirteen, fifteen, and sixteen. Also recently, two sixteen-year-olds in Iowa stalked and killed their sixty-six-year-old Spanish teacher while she was out for her daily exercise routine. Violent crime by juveniles remains a persistent social challenge.

I have to conclude that we simply don't have a handle on our problems, that we are losing our grip. Our responses seem slipshod and ill-conceived. I watched in dismay from afar when San Francisco elected a progressive district attorney, Chas Boudin, a son of the sixties in more ways than one. His parents, Kathy Boudin and David Gilbert, were Weather Underground activists convicted in the murder of two police officers and a security guard. As a DA, Chas Boudin's policies were straight out of the anti-law enforcement playbook of the radical sixties.

The experiment did not work out well. Gaining office after promoting a platform of reducing incarceration and criminal justice reform, Boudin stumbled badly. Not one, but two recall campaigns targeted him, and led to his removal from office. His office was plagued by disorganization and high turnover. While he had his eyes on the progressive prize, he left unattended the vital, day-to-day functions of ensuring public safety and prosecuting crime.

"I cannot express in any more certain terms my disapproval of the manner in which the Office of the District Attorney is being managed," San Francisco Superior Court Judge Bruce Chan commented. "Not to make light of the situation, but you can't run an airline this way."[4]

Chan continued, "I hope people in the District Attorney's Office will shift their focus from some of the bigger issues and concern themselves with the unglamorous yet necessary work of public prosecution. It's time to really take care of business at home instead of thinking about the national or state stage."[5]

There it is, perfectly expressed. While putting forth their idealistic, big-picture reforms, progressive prosecutors have lost sight of "the unglamorous yet necessary work of public prosecution."

The Chas Boudin debacle in San Francisco isn't the only case of progressive prosecutors gone wrong. Los Angeles District Attorney George Gascón also faced recall efforts due to his wrong-headed policies. High-profile killings, "follow-home" robberies, and smash-and-grab store invasions prompted the campaign to remove Gascón from office.

Closer to home, and closer to my heart since it involves DANY, is the rocky start to the term in office of Alvin Bragg, who was elected as New York County District Attorney in November 2021. On his first day in office he immediately instituted a slate of

---

4 Jay Barmann, "The People, Plaintiff and Respondent, v. Jeffrey Brent Shackelford" (court transcript, *San Francisco Examiner*, August 2019).

5 Ibid.

progressive reforms that backfired spectacularly. In an infamous "Day One" memo, Bragg announced that his office would no longer prosecute low-level offenses unless they were accompanied by a felony charge.

In another "reform" that violated the fundamental principle of ensuring public safety, Bragg stated that his office would seek lesser charges for burglaries and store robberies where the offender "displays a dangerous instrument but does not create a genuine risk of physical harm." He also put in place a "presumption of non-incarceration" in all cases that came before DANY.

The default position of the office, in other words, would be to put criminals back on the streets. In reality, his policies created a get-out-of-jail-free card for criminals. Why would a robber, burglar, or other criminal commit a crime in Staten Island, the Bronx, Queens, or Brooklyn where, if convicted, they could go to state prison, when they could do it in Manhattan without the fear of being incarcerated?

The outrage from the public was immediate and vocal. Pushback came from the mayor, the business community, and the NYPD—including objections voiced by the newly appointed Police Commissioner, Keechant L. Sewell, the first woman and the third African-American to hold the position.

Bragg found himself walking back many of his policy changes. His claim that his policies would make Manhattan communities safer and stronger was nothing more than a pipe dream. I am pessimistic about the future of the office I served and loved for such a long time, the rigorous, effective, and celebrated institution that Frank Hogan and Robert Morgenthau worked so long and hard to create.

I have the sense that the Boss—my boss, Robert Morgenthau, the man who is credited with being the best Manhattan DA of all time—would be turning over in his grave. I hear of widespread discontent within the office, with defections by top-quality ADAs unhappy with the direction their new boss has embarked upon.

On the surface, the progressive platform embraces laudable goals: reforming the criminal justice system to ensure that all individuals are treated fairly, reforming the bail system, and reducing the prison population by diverting low level offenders from jail into programs that will help them become productive, law-abiding citizens. Also, based on the shooting deaths of so many people of color, there is a self-evident need to better train the police and hold them accountable.

The plain fact is that these progressive policies have not made our communities safer. Lately, with the increase of violent crime throughout the country, the cry of defunding the police has gone silent. As seen in Manhattan, Los Angeles, and San Francisco, the idealistic policies of progressive prosecutors have been proven to be unrealistic in reducing crime and keeping dangerous criminals off the street.

I see what's happening in America right now with a fear of where we are headed and a sense of having been there before. We risk making the same mistakes all over again, plunging society into a nightmare of drugs and violence.

I fully realize that the viewpoint of a prosecutor isn't the be-all and end-all in the public dialogue on crime, violence, and drug use. But all too often it is dismissed from the discussion entirely. It's vital that the voice of law enforcement be heard.

It has now been over twenty-five years since I left SNP, and the drug landscape has changed. I am concerned about the recent movement to legalize hard, addictive drugs. Across the country, voters have spoken. In the November 2020 elections, every measure on state ballots aimed at legalizing drugs or reforming drug laws won the approval of voters. The initiatives passed by wide margins. The results at the polls represented a clear mandate to end century-old prohibitionist drug policies. The resulting "green wave" of drug legalization legislation prompts a question not of the past but of the future. What happens now?

As I witness the current wave of drug legalization initiatives, I remind myself that we already have a cautionary example of what happens when legalized drugs get unleashed upon the American public.

We don't have to wonder. We already know all too well, because there is a narcotics plague sweeping up communities, families, adults, and children all over the country. Right now, there is a contemporary, high-profile example that should make the consequences of drug legalization obvious to all. The tragic, unforeseen repercussions are out there in the open for everyone to see. Like many drug plagues throughout our nation's history, this one began with a substance that was perfectly legal to obtain and use: prescription opioids.

For over a quarter century now, the opioid epidemic has been an evolving crisis in American life. The accelerating catastrophe kicked into high gear with the introduction of a drug trademarked as Oxycontin in 1995, a highly effective painkiller if used appropriately. Since Oxycontin featured a supposed time-release function, the drug was originally marketed as an opioid painkiller that was somehow magically addiction-proof. However, the approval of the drug for medical applications legalized the widespread use of a dangerously addictive opioid. A doctor's prescription was necessary, of course, but from the beginning the medical establishment wrote scripts as if they were afraid of running out of ink. In 2017 alone, healthcare providers dispensed 191 million prescriptions for opioid pain medication, a rate of almost sixty prescriptions per one hundred people.

Oxycontin enjoyed huge popularity exactly because it was a legal drug. It was a legitimate painkiller, and didn't have anything to do with junkies, "cooking up," or drug dens. Physicians said it was okay, so it had to be okay, right? Like the old line about the first dose of heroin or the first marijuana cigarette being "free," the first use of "Oxy" was free—literally free, because insurance companies covered its cost, but also free from the unsavory associations of heroin use.

But users were not "druggies," were they? They were patients. Actually, given the relentless marketing campaign behind Oxycontin, they were not patients at all, but consumers. Suffering in the excruciatingly painful aftermath of surgery, say, a person might rationalize use of the drug. "Okay, I can get a prescription, right? There's nothing wrong with that. I'm not committing a crime. I'm getting drugs legally."

We all witnessed what happened next, and what is still happening due to the widespread use of these heavily promoted, perfectly legal drugs. When their Oxycontin prescriptions ran out, addicted users resorted to buying pills on the black market, or they moved sideways to other, cheaper opioids. People died. People fell into the agony of addiction. Crime escalated. Whole communities crumbled.

Oxycontin was developed legally, manufactured legally, licensed for sale legally, marketed legally, and sold legally. This opioid should be considered as a prime example of drug legalization.

Oxycontin stands as a flashing red warning signal amid the rush to decriminalize formerly banned substances. It has killed hundreds of thousands of people, and it's not over yet. Much of America remains in crisis because of the abuse of a legal drug.

During the current debate over drug legalization, I feel an unreal sense that the public, legislators, and media commentators miss a basic fact. It's like the proverbial eight-hundred pound gorilla no one talks about, or the elephant in the room everyone ignores. Users of legal drugs are dying in numbers that rival the mortality figures of the coronavirus pandemic. Where is the all-hands-on-deck response? Other than civil lawsuits, which the manufacturers have lost, and doctors cutting down on prescriptions, what is the federal government doing to help stop this crisis?

Instead, in our infinite wisdom we seem to be going the opposite way. With the push toward legalization, we want to unleash more, not fewer, legal drugs into our communities.

I want to grab the public by its lapels and shout, "Don't you see?"

Throughout my career I've seen hauntingly similar drug plagues. As Yogi Berra used to say, "it's déjà vu all over again." Or, to use a more intellectual quotation from the German philosopher Hegel, "The only thing we learn from history is that we do not learn from history."

I was on the front lines of that history during the crack epidemic of the 1980s and 1990s. Crack cocaine was an illegal schedule one narcotic, so there are obvious differences with what is happening today. We are not seeing the levels of violent criminal activity associated with the drug wars that we did during the 80s and 90s. The arrest rate for narcotic violations is way down. Drug abuse fatalities, however, are higher. The opioid epidemic has gotten only limited levels of legal attention, mostly because of the civil lawsuits that were brought against pharmaceutical companies and won.

The abuse of Oxycontin represents another example of the insatiable appetite for Americans to obtain and use drugs. The zealous determination of my fellow citizens to get high aston-ished me at first, but long ago I became inured to it. We in the U.S. constitute under five percent of the world's population, but consume two-thirds of the world's illegal drugs and eighty percent of the world's opioids. We might be on our way to becoming the legalization nation, but we are already the addiction nation.

In the 1990s, when I served as New York City's Special Narcotics Prosecutor, Felix Jimenez, then the second-in-command of the Drug Enforcement Administration's New York Office, requested a meeting.

"The Colombians are getting into the heroin business now," he informed me. Formerly concentrating on supplying cocaine to world markets, the powerful Colombian drug cartels had branched out.

"The product is much more potent and powerful," Jimenez warned me. "It's so pure that users don't have to inject it. They can just snort it for the rush."

We have, today, an eerily identical situation with fentanyl. Fentanyl is a synthetic molecule, which as a medicine and pain-killer has been around since 1960, when a pioneering chemist named Paul Janssen first formulated it. Its use in anesthesia proved miraculous. If you've had a colonoscopy, you've probably taken fentanyl legally.

The nightmare came later.

Originally manufactured in large quantities in China, the extremely potent opioid has now migrated to the cartels of South and Central America. In the Mexican province of Sinaloa, where fentanyl is called "black goat," the high-potency narcotic is cooked up from precursors by home-trained chemists using primitive methods. No one needs a lab or a pharmacology degree.

Paul Janssen had only the best intentions. Throughout his career he sought tirelessly to relieve physical pain in all its manifestations. But his best intentions paved the way to the hellish American landscape of today, where a pinprick-sized dose of fentanyl can result in an overdose and death.

A tiny dose is enough to kill. Ask the mother of thirteen-year-old Luca Manuel, a victim of a fatal overdose. The teen accessed the drug off the web, and his mom had a brief chance to embrace her son's dead body before the arrival of the coroner. Similar is the case of Alex Capelouto. She came home from college for the holidays, but died before Christmas from a counterfeit prescription pill laced with fentanyl. Most recently, the death of a one-year-old who was exposed to fentanyl fumes in his day care center in the Bronx, which garnered national attention.

"It was as easy as ordering a pizza, delivered right to our house," Alex's father, Max Capelouto, said of online access to such fatal illicit meds.

Now Fentanyl has the potential of becoming a killer many times more dangerous than any substance that has come before. It is so powerful, and so fast-acting, that junkies are often discovered dead with the hypodermic needle still impaled in their arms. It has been turning up in any number of street drug admixtures, providing a boost in the strength of cocaine, meth, and ecstasy. Casual drug users can no longer be sure what they are about to ingest—a drug-induced high or a fatal dose? Merciless drug dealers now market fentanyl as candy-colored pills, not caring if they attract or kill children. It has gotten so bad that recently fentanyl test strips were developed so users can make sure their drugs are safe.

The usual arguments advanced in support of legalization most often include: (1) current drug laws have failed to eradicate the drug problem; (2) the "war on drugs" has been lost, and it is time to acknowledge that defeat; (3) arresting and incarcerating people who should not be in jail does nothing to alleviate the drug problem, simply wreaking havoc on the lives of those incarcerated and their families; (4) drug crimes are victimless crimes; (5) legalization will lead to a reduction in drug-related crimes and violence; and (6) precious resources have been wasted on law enforcement initiatives that do not even begin to solve the drug problem.

Over the years, I have heard those arguments repeatedly. Based on my experience, I believe that anyone who argues that the legalization of hard drugs is a panacea for our drug problems is not only wrong, but is advocating a cure worse than the disease.

Legalization will not reduce the number of individuals who use controlled substances. Instead, it promises to increase that number by removing the existing sanctions that undoubtedly deter at least some from using drugs. At the same time, legalization appears to place society's imprimatur on drug use.

But let us suppose we do decide to legalize drugs. Do we legalize all drugs, including cocaine, fentanyl, and heroin? And whether we legalize some or all drugs, do we impose age limitations on those who may use the drugs, setting an age limit of twenty-one years, for example, or eighteen, or ten? If we legalize some drugs and at the same time impose age limitations, the existing black market for illegal drugs will focus on selling the drugs not legalized and on selling drugs (legal and illegal) to those below the age limit.

This black market will inevitably result in the same kind of violence that illegal trafficking now inflicts upon society. Drug gangs and drug dealers will continue to plague our cities, which will continue to decay as residents flee, seeking safety outside those cities.

Legalization is not the answer. It is surrender.

In response to the argument that the "war on drugs" has been lost, I ask: "What war?" The sad fact is that, although there have been attacks, skirmishes, battles, and encounters, there has never been a "war on drugs" in any meaningful way. The "war on drugs" has never been more than a slogan belied by the facts.

By studying the annals of WWII, we've seen how a well-conducted war must be fought. In that case, the whole country mobilized. War requires a national commitment, a recognition that the enemy threatens the health and welfare of the nation, and a well-thought-out, cohesive strategy.

Society as a whole must recognize that the "war on drugs" must be fought on many fronts, including education, treatment, and law enforcement. We need to employ all the resources necessary to defeat the enemy. If, as people customarily claim, we have been fighting a "war on drugs," then the necessary commitment, strategy, and employment of resources have all been missing in action, and our leaders have been derelict in their duty.

We need a national commitment to deal with the scourge of illicit drugs because the damage inflicted by drug abuse is a nationwide problem. It is true that the drug laws have failed to eradicate our drug problem. But we've been naive to have ever believed that simply putting in place laws prohibiting the use and sale of controlled substances could eradicate our drug problem.

To defeat the enemy requires a strategy that recognizes that the drug war has many theaters of engagement. It involves not only the enforcement of existing drug laws, but huge increases in educational programs and drug treatment and rehabilitation facilities. Instead, the so-called war on drugs has been fought piecemeal.

There have been some notable successes. In the early years of the millennium, America experienced a nationwide reduction in crime, in large measure due to the targeted, sustained, and coordinated efforts of law enforcement in dismantling violent drug gangs.

Since those successes have led to a reduction in media coverage of the drug problem, I am more pessimistic than ever that the necessary national commitment will arise. In the years since I retired from SNP, we don't see any more coverage of press conferences that feature arrays of confiscated drugs, guns, and money piled upon a table in front of law enforcement personnel and prosecutors. Where drug stories once occupied the front pages of the newspapers, they are now relegated to the back pages.

Apart from the opioid crisis, and more recently fentanyl, it appears that the drug problem is being discussed less and less. Indeed, the drug issue received scant attention during the 2020 presidential election. It has finally become an issue during the 2024 presidential cycle, only as it regards the border crisis and the importation of fentanyl into the country. There is no real ongoing national discussion. In addition, there has been a lack of interaction and a lack of coordination of efforts between those involved in law enforcement and those involved in education, treatment, and rehabilitation.

As an important first step in fighting a real war on drugs, I would convene a national drug summit. Composed of leading educators, drug experts, law enforcement personnel, businesspeople, and representatives of the media and entertainment industry, the summit would be charged with developing and formulating an intelligent, all-encompassing drug policy.

Answers to the following questions should be of paramount importance: What are the most effective educational tools available, and how can they be best employed to prevent children and young adults from using drugs? What treatment programs, in and out of prisons, have been most effective in helping addicts recover? What diversion programs exist, or can be devised, that offer a viable alternative to prison for nonviolent drug dealers who sell to support a habit? What law enforcement initiatives offer the best hope of keeping drugs out of the country and reducing drug-related violence in our neighborhoods?

Of course, an intelligent drug policy is meaningless in the absence of a strong national commitment. Educational programs, treatment programs, diversion programs, and law enforcement require substantial resources. A national commitment requires leadership, vision, dedication, and a wise and generous commitment of resources as well. That leadership must come from Washington—from the president and Congress. The states simply do not have the resources or power to combat a national drug epidemic.

To date, leadership from the federal government has been in short supply. "Leadership and vision" is not a catchy slogan, and paying lip service to the problem is not the same as dedication. The federal government's track record, even in those areas that do not require tax funds, has been disappointing. Much more can be done to enlist the media, business, and the entertainment industry in broadcasting the message that drugs are harmful and not socially acceptable.

When it comes to the drug problem, the federal government has failed to meet its obligation to "insure domestic tranquility, provide for the common defense, and promote the general welfare." When this nation was embroiled in the Civil War, President Abraham Lincoln took command, vowing to preserve the Union. When this nation plummeted into the Great Depression, President Franklin Roosevelt took charge, promising to lift the nation out of its economic crisis.

Neither Lincoln nor Roosevelt had any simple answers. They had vision, dedication, and the willingness and determination to use all the resources necessary to succeed. With this nation's cities blighted by drugs, Nancy Reagan told the nation to "Just Say No," and the impotent office of the Drug Czar was created. When the opioid epidemic descended upon the country, killing thousands, Washington was asleep at the switch. If the effort to send a man to the moon had suffered under the same lack of national commitment as the so-called war on drugs, Apollo 11 would never have left the launch pad.

The wide-ranging impulse to decriminalize and legalize hard drugs is the kind of knee-jerk response that is less an answer than a defeated, throwing-up-of-hands when confronting a complex challenge. It will not solve the problem, but instead will aggravate it. Only a focused, nationwide policy will do the job, combining interdiction of illicit substances and prosecution of criminal organizations, along with social programs that address addiction, violence, and abuse.

We have mounted "moon shot" initiatives before to cure cancer or to develop vaccines in the face of a pandemic. The problem of overdose deaths, drug violence, and use of illicit narcotics is severe enough to require a similar coordinated, nationwide response. We owe it to our families, our children, and ourselves.

ABOUT THE AUTHOR

Robert Silbering joined the Manhattan District Attorney's office in 1974 and left in 1997. While still a Manhattan Assistant District Attorney, he was assigned to the Special Narcotics Prosecutor's Office in 1984, where he was the Chief Assistant. When the Special Prosecutor was appointed as a federal judge by President George H. W. Bush in 1991, Silbering was appointed by the five New York City District Attorneys to replace the Special Prosecutor.

In 1997, he left Special Narcotics to become the President of Forensic Investigative Associates (FIA), USA. He headed up the U.S. operations of an international investigative and consulting firm. He later became a Senior Vice President of Investigations at T&M Protection Resources, a firm that specializes in security and investigations. Today, Silbering is the Special Advisor to the CEO of the company. Although he is more involved in investigations, at times he has become involved in legal matters where he is appointed by a court to be a monitor of a company or a Trustee of a company.

He lives in New York with his wife.

BIBLIOGRAPHY

Anderson, David C. "The Editorial Notebook; How to Rescue a Crack House," *The New York Times*, February 8, 1993. https://www.nytimes.com/1993/02/08/opinion/the-editorial-notebook-how-to-rescue-a-crack-house.html (accessed September 24, 2023).

Barmann, Jay. "The People, Plaintiff and Respondent, v. Jeffrey Brent Shackelford." Court transcript, *San Francisco Examiner*, August 2019.

Collins, Jim. *Good to Great* (New York, NY: Harper Business 2001).

Snyder, Leslie, Tom Shachtman. *25 to Life: The Truth, The Whole Truth, and Nothing But the Truth* (New York, NY: Warmer Books, 2002), 311.